F-5

TIGERS OVER VIETNAM

By

Anthony J. Tambini

228 9th Lane

South San Francisco, CA 94080

Telephone: (650)-588-4178

E-mail: tglb8@aol.com

Contents

Southeast Asia Countries in Conflict

Preface

Over the past several decades, the air war over Vietnam has been told primarily from the United States Military perspective. The war in the air was fought using a wide range of U.S. operated aircraft that encompassed everything from the Mach three SR-71 Blackbird, to the extremely subsonic single engine piston powered light observation aircraft such as the Cessna O-1. U.S. airborne operations have been well documented. The gallantry of the airmen assigned the difficult task of operating not only over the jungles of Vietnam, but also over the most sophisticated air defense system ever encountered in combat is legendary.

However, not well documented is the story of the Republic of Vietnam Air Force, better known at that time as the VNAF. The South Vietnamese Air Force during the 1950s and early 1960s was a collection of aircraft that dated back to World War Two. All the aircraft in the South Vietnamese inventory were piston powered, slow and old. Up until the mid-1960s the South Vietnamese were conducting combat operations with such aircraft as the propeller driven A-1 Skyraider, an aircraft that entered U.S. service during the Korean War.

The VNAF came of age with the introduction of a revolutionary aircraft developed by the Northrop Corporation, the F-5 Freedom Fighter. The F-5 was a supersonic fighter-bomber developed for the export market. In a time when fighter-bombers had grown in size, complexity and costs, the F-5 was a godsend to countries that needed a combat aircraft that they could economically fly and maintain.

The F-5 fit the bill beyond expectations. It could be operated at a fraction of the cost and manpower that were the hallmarks of U.S. fighter and attack aircraft of the time. Easy to maintain and effective as an attack aircraft, it came at a time when the VNAF desperately needed such an aircraft for their fledgling combat fleet.

An eyewitness to events in South Vietnam tells this story. The author worked directly with South Vietnamese pilots and ground crewmembers from May of 1972 through April 01 1975. This then is something rare among aviation books about the South Vietnamese Air Force, as it is told by actual on-site observation. All photos in this book are from the author's collection.

Chapter 1

Development of the Freedom Fighter

The Northrop Corporation has always been known as an aviation innovator. The company designed and produced the first U.S. aircraft designed from the ground up as a night fighter. This aircraft, the P-61 Black Widow, gave the Army Air Force an airborne radar platform for conducting night attacks on enemy warplanes over the European Continent as well as the Pacific theater of operations. During the early 1950s the company was responsible for the first jet interceptor specifically designed for air defense, dedicated to the protection of the U.S. mainland. That aircraft was the F-89 Scorpion, a two-place aircraft that carried a pilot and a radar observer. It was designed to shoot down the vast fleets of in-coming enemy bombers that, at the time, were perceived as the most likely airborne threat to the country. Also during the early to mid-1950s the company was working on a truly novel concept, a supersonic cruise missile capable of carrying a nuclear warhead. Named the Snark, the company worked tirelessly with the U.S. Air Force in developing this capability.

This innovative foresight carried forward, when in 1954 the company sent a team of savvy individuals on a tour of our European and Asian allies. The intent of the company sponsored tour was to canvass our allies to better determine their specific needs as related to that of a potentially new fighter aircraft. Northrop soon realized that the most pressing need of our allies was an affordable and easily maintained combat aircraft capable of both air to air as well as air to ground operations. Throughout the 1950s the U.S. military operated a wide range of combat aircraft that, as far as our allies were concerned, were either too old, or in the case of newer aircraft, too costly to operate and maintain.

The results of the team's findings led Northrop on a quest to develop a fighter aircraft that could truly meet the needs of our allies. The genesis was a 1955 company funded project known as the N-156 Lightweight Fighter Program. Affordability and performance were to be evenly matched goals of the program. Supersonic performance was to be attained with an affordable lightweight jet engine that was a derivative of an engine powering a cruise missile of the era. The General Electric J-85-GE-1 non-afterburning jet engine powering the GAM-72 Quail missile was selected to power the new N-156 fighter. This engine produced a total of 2100 pounds of thrust, which although sufficient to propel the small Quail missile, was insufficient for the supersonic performance of the new fighter. What Northrop envisioned was an afterburning version producing more thrust. General Electric decided that it could produce a version of this engine capable of approximately 3,800 pounds of thrust in afterburner. With G.E. working on the engine, Northrop continued its quest for the supersonic N-156.

The fruits of this labor paid off when in mid-1955 the single seat N-156 and dual seat N-156F designs were finalized. Northrop submitted its lightweight fighter proposal to both the U.S. Air Force and Navy. The Navy had absolutely no interest in the aircraft. The Air Force also had no interest in the lightweight fighter for its own use, however it viewed the two-seat N-156F as a potential candidate for a trainer aircraft it had planned to replace the aging subsonic Lockheed T-33 jet trainer.

In late 1955 the Air Force issued General Operating Requirement number SS-240, setting forth the requirements the service needed for a new trainer aircraft to replace the T-33. In June of 1956 the Northrop N-156F was selected as meeting the needs of the Air Force. The service re-designated the aircraft the T-38 and named it the Talon. The first prototype T-38A flew in April of 1958. Although it was not the aircraft Northrop initially intended to manufacture, the company eventually produced a total of 1,189 of the unarmed supersonic T-38A Talon trainers for the USAF. Company funded work continued on the N-156, work that refined the original design.

Beginning with the start of the Korean War, the USAF and USN had placed greater and greater emphasis on large sophisticated aircraft for combat in Europe against the Warsaw Pact countries. The USAF became increasingly aware of the need for an affordable fighter for its allies, and in late 1958 expressed an interest in the N-156. Based on consent and funding from the Air Force, three prototypes were built. The prototypes were called Freedom Fighters and given military serial numbers 59-4987, 59-4988 and 59-4989. Although the first Freedom Fighter to be flown (59-4987) was powered by twin non-afterburning GE-J-85-1 engines, it flew supersonic on its first flight.

Testing of the Freedom Fighter was accomplished at Edwards AFB, located in California's high desert. All three prototypes were fitted with afterburning engines for the Air Force testing. Live firings of infrared guided Sidewinder and Falcon missiles validated the Freedom Fighters air-to-air capabilities. Air-to-ground testing included the dropping of live 250, 500 and 750-pound bombs. Testing was also accomplished on accurate delivery of napalm canisters and the firing of 2.75-inch folding fin rockets from under wing pods capable of up to 24 rockets per pod. Rough field operations were also conducted, with the aircraft successfully operating from dirt strips. Also tested was a novel concept, for fighters at least, of getting the aircraft airborne with rocket assisted take-off bottles. These were required for customers operating from relatively high airfields, such as in the mountainous areas of the Andes in South America.

During this testing the U.S. Army expressed a desire to acquire the aircraft for its small fixed wing air arm. A series of operational tests were conducted, with at least on aircraft painted olive-drab with U.S. Army stenciled in bold letters on the sides of its fuselage. The Army had seen great potential in the little aircraft. Unfortunately the Air Force put an abrupt end politically to this plan.

To Northrop's great relief, in April of 1962 the Department of Defense selected the N-156 as its Military Assistance Program (MAP) aircraft for worldwide use in allied air forces. In August of that year the Air Force re-designated the model from the company N-156 to the military fighter designation F-5A, retaining the Freedom Fighter name. A two-seat version was also authorized for production, this version would bear the F-5B designation (second in the series). The initial production contract for 71 aircraft was granted in October of 1962. A follow-on contract for 99 aircraft was issued in August of 1963. Both contracts were for a mix of A and B model aircraft in a ratio of one F-5B to each nine F-5As. Twelve aircraft per month were planned, with the first delivery scheduled to take place during the first quarter of 1965.

The prototypes and initial batch of production aircraft were not configured to carry guns. This was somewhat typical thinking of the time. With the advent of infrared and radar guided missiles, the concept of a modern day fighter with a gun seemed outmoded to military planners. The McDonnell F-4 Phantom II was a good example of this thinking. The F-4 was designed in the mid-1950s and performed its first flight in 1958. When it was originally designed, a gun was omitted. The thinking of the time was that for long range intercepts, the AIM-7 Sparrow radar guided missile would kill the enemy aircraft. For short range work, the AIM-9B infrared missile would do the trick. Guns were definitely passé and not very high tech. In the late 1960s, and the advent of air combat over Vietnam, the F-4E would emerge from the McDonnell stable sporting a chin mounted Gatling gun. In 1964 the

USAF added an operational requirement to the F-5 incorporating two 20mm M-39A cannons into the nose of the aircraft. Weapons aiming were accomplished via cues provided by the ranging set and displayed on an optical sight in line with the pilot's vision in the cockpit. Although not equipped with a radar directed fire control system, weapons were aimed with a radar ranging set mounted in the nose of the aircraft. Weapons aiming were accomplished via cues provided by the ranging set and displayed on an optical sight in line with the pilot's vision in the cockpit. This was a very low cost but effective method of placing weapons on target. The F-5B did not have the M-39 cannons incorporated into its design. This was due to the fact that the addition of the second cockpit precluded the installation of the guns. The design simply would not allow for the installation due to the requirement to maintain as much commonality with the F-5A. The addition of the guns to the F-5B would have meant lengthening the aircraft considerably. The "B" model was designated primarily as a trainer aircraft, however it did retain the capability to drop ordnance.

Norway was actually the first overseas customer to order the F-5, with a contract let for 64 aircraft in February of 1964. This sale set the stag for the little lightweight fighter to enter the international market as the first affordable modern fighter/attack aircraft that many foreign governments could afford not only to possess but also to operate and maintain.

The U.S. government, seeking to replace the aging hodgepodge mix of aircraft operated by the Republic of Vietnam Air Force (VNAF), looked anew at the performance of Northrop's wonder fighter. Providing a supersonic fighter/bomber to the VNAF would benefit not only the prosecution of the war, but also boost the morale of VNAF personnel and the South Vietnamese in general.

The Department of Defense (DOD) decided in late1964 to dispatch a squadron of Freedom Fighters to Vietnam to test the aircraft in actual combat. Northrop's gamble on the novel idea of an effective, affordable and maintainable fighter for foreign governments was about to make its combat debut. The DODs first though decided that the aircraft must be tested under controlled conditions to ensure it was specifically what was needed. A test evaluation called Project Sparrow Hawk was conducted at the USAF Tactical Air Warfare Center at Eglin Air Force Base in Florida. The original intent of the project was to evaluate the A-6A, A-4E and F-5A to determine if the military could actually use such a fighter as the F-5A. The A-6A was withdrawn from the project and the A-4C was substituted. Five F-5A aircraft took part in this test and evaluation.

During the testing, the USAF proposed that the F-5A might be procured under the Military Assistance Program (MAP) for operations with the Vietnamese Air Force. The DOD acted upon the proposal; a plan was developed and put forth for the testing of the aircraft in actual combat. This proposal leads to the Skoshi Tiger Combat Evaluation Program.

Chapter 2

USAF Skoshi Tiger Operations

In South Vietnam

(Skoshi - Japanese for small)

In October of 1965 the USAF acquired twelve F-5As from Military Assistance Program inventory and assigned them to the 4503rd Tactical Fighter Squadron (Provisional) for operational testing. The 4503rd was formed on 26 July 1965 at Williams Air Force Base in Arizona. The unit was commissioned to perform operational testing and to train pilots and mechanics on the F-5 aircraft. Williams AFB, in the Arizona desert, was an ideal site for conducting flight operations, as clear skies prevailed most days of the year. The Skoshi Tiger program was originally known as the Sparrow Hawk Program. The designation Sparrow Hawk was changed to Skoshi Tiger when the original plan for a lightweight, easily maintainable fighter was completed and forwarded to Secretary of Defense McNamara.

Army General William Westmoreland had initially asked for twenty-five of the lightweight fighters for the VNAF. Secretary of Defense McNamara was not enthusiastic about this and recommended the delivery of F-5s for the VNAF be delayed until after a combat evaluation could be completed. An additional concern McNamara had was the drain of air force units from Europe to fight in the Southeast Asia conflict. This made the turnover of F-5s to the VNAF less attractive. One USAF squadron of F-5s in Vietnam meant the retention of one squadron of more sophisticated aircraft could remain in the European theater.

The twelve F-5As assigned to the 4503rd were modified by Northrop at its Palmdale, California facility. The modifications were to incorporate the necessary items of equipment to support combat operations overseas. In-flight refueling probes were added to each aircraft for the long over water flight to Southeast Asia and also, if required, for extending air operations within the war zone. Ninety pounds of lead armor plating was mounted externally to the underside of each aircraft. This plating was positioned under the cockpit for pilot protection and also under the engine/accessory area for aircraft survivability. An optical lead computing gun sight was added to better improve weapons accuracy. Jettisonable external stores pylons were also added to improve the survivability of the aircraft in combat. The aircraft initially incorporated a rudder limiter to prevent excessive rudder deflections at high speeds. The rudder limiter was removed as part of the modification program, providing the pilot with greater maneuverability. Also included as part of the modification was the installation of a more stabilized, reliable weapons delivery platform. To top off the modification program, the aircraft were painted in typical Southeast Asia green/tan camouflage. The aircraft passed the operational evaluation and went into a short maintenance period to ensure each was mechanically ready for the long over water flight and multiple air refueling into South Vietnam. With the addition of the in-flight refueling capability the aircraft were re-designated as F-5Cs.

The aircraft deployed from Williams AFB and flew to Hickam AFB in Hawaii. The flight lasted a total of six hours and required eight in-flight refueling. After a short stay in Hawaii, the aircraft took off for the second leg of the long journey.

The second portion of the deployment sent the aircraft to Andersen AFB on the island of Guam. Stops at Wake and Midway islands were made for inspection and servicing. This portion of the trip took eight hours and required five in-flight refueling and covered a distance of 3,429 miles. The next leg took the aircraft from Guam to Clark Air Base in the Philippians and then into Bien Hoa Air Base, South Vietnam.

This last leg covered 2,256 miles, took five hours and required three in-flight refueling link ups. Total distance covered during the trip was 8,279 nautical miles in 19 flying hours.

On October 23rd, the twelve Freedom Fighters landed at Bien Hoa Air Base in South Vietnam. Five hours after arrival, two of the aircraft were flying air operations in combat areas of war zone D, in the southern portion of South Vietnam. Three aircraft were scheduled on this mission, however one ground aborted with engine afterburner difficulties.

The two aircraft were armed with four 500-pound bombs and a complete load of 500-rounds of 20mm cannon ammunition. Intelligence had reported that a Viet Cong battalion, with an estimated strength of 500 men, was in the target area. The two F-5s made five bombing passes, dropped two tons of bombs directly on the target and then proceeded to strafe the area with cannon fire.

As a point of reference, Bien Hoa city and the air base, are located approximately 30 miles northwest of what was at the time called Saigon, the capital of the former South Vietnam. The city of Saigon had its name changed to Ho Chi Minh City during the reunification that took place after the 1975 fall of the government of South Vietnam. Bien Hoa air base was host to the Vietnam Air Forces 3rd Air Division. The 3rd Air Division was responsible for VNAF air operations over most of military region III.

Although developed as a fighter, the F-5s performed primarily in the attack roll, conducting air-to-ground operations while in-country. The combat evaluation originally was also designed to compare the F-5 to other USAF in-country jet fighter/attack aircraft. The comparisons would be with the F-100 Super Sabers from the 12th Tactical Fighter Wing at Bien Hoa and F-104 Starfighters assigned to the 435th Tactical Fighter Squadron at Da Nang Air Base in the northern portion of the country. The F-104s were dropped from the comparisons when they departed Vietnam for Thailand in November of 1965. In early December of 1965 the F-4C Phantom II became fully operational with the USAF at Cam Rahn Air Base and it was then decided to add the F-4 to the comparison tasking, taking the place of the recently departed F-104s. (See appendix 1 for a listing of Skoshi Tiger serial numbers assigned to the evaluation).

Accompanying the Skoshi Tigers was a team of 33 evaluators tasked to monitor the aircraft for maintainability, survivability and accuracy of weapons delivery. To keep the evaluation as "real life" as possible, F-5s were integrated into combat operations in Vietnam and treated like any other available weapons system. The F-5 squadron fell under the responsibility of the USAF 2nd Air Division, which planned operations for all air assets in the war zone. The actual maintenance team consisted of a total of 175 USAF maintenance technicians. Manpower wise, this was an extremely small number of maintenance technicians when compared to an aircraft like the McDonnell F-4C.

The in-country combat evaluation was divided into three phases. Phase one was to be a 60-day evaluation of the aircraft in a combat environment. The squadron was to work with forward air and ground controllers in accurately placing ordnance on requested targets. Phase two would dispatch aircraft to a forward location to conduct combat air patrols. These were fighter operations designed to protect the skies over the country from enemy aircraft. Phase two would also be tasked to support ground operations if requested. Phase three was a accelerated combat sortie generation rate test. During this phase, a small number of aircraft would conduct from 20 to 30 combat operations per day for a designated period of days.

Phase one lasted 66 days. A total of 1,500 combat sorties were flown with the twelve aircraft assigned to the evaluation. Over three-million pounds of ordnance was delivered to targets in southern South Vietnam. Forward air and ground controllers reported excellent weapons deliveries during this phase. Unfortunately, one aircraft was lost to enemy ground fire. Aircraft damaged during combat averaged on hit by ground fire per 26 combat sorties. The damaging ground fire was usually sustained after the aircraft delivered ordnance on the target and were pulling up and away after the bombing run. All repairs during this phase of testing were accomplished overnight with the aircraft being completely mission capable the next day.

On November 24, 1965 South Vietnamese Air Force Marshal General Nguyen Cao Ky visited Bien Hoa air base with the specific intention of seeing the aircraft and men. He received an on-site briefing on how the combat evaluation was proceeding. The visit also included a detailed briefing on the mission and operations of the squadron. The General was reported to have been very impressed with the aircraft. The flamboyant General later was checked out in the F-5B and reportedly loved the aircraft.

On December 5th, 1965 the commander of the 4503rd, Colonel Frank N. Emery, flew the squadron's 1,000th combat mission. Later the Colonel briefed squadron personnel on the performance of the aircraft and on how well the evaluation was progressing. Being in a combat environment and being away from family and friends, all members of the team were appreciative of the briefing and on being informed on how well the aircraft was performing.

On the 7th of December a milestone of sorts was passed when aircraft serial number 64-13318 flew its 100th combat mission. This was the first F-5A to reach the 100-mission mark and was flown by Major Joseph B. Baggett. The aircraft was part of a three aircraft sortie on a ground support mission approximately twenty miles west of Saigon. The flight destroyed twelve structures and damaged nineteen others.

Unfortunately, Major Baggett was to lose his life a few days later while flying a combat support mission on December 16th. Major Baggett was flying aircraft serial number 63-8425 on a close air support mission approximately fifteen miles west of Saigon when enemy ground fire hit his aircraft. The aircraft became uncontrollable and he ejected from the crippled jet. Although he was later rescued by a U.S. Army helicopter, sadly he passed away from his injuries.

A review of operations and maintenance at the end of phase one shed some interesting light on the aircraft. Pilots and maintenance technicians loved the aircraft. It was determined that the squadron's planes flew, on the average, 24 sorties a day. This equated to two sorties per aircraft per day. It was also determined that they the aircraft were capable of flying at least twice that number. Mechanics loved how easy it was to work on the lightweight fighters. Pilots had somewhat mixed emotions of the aircraft. They praised the flying and handling qualities, and the fact that the aircraft was not only supersonic, small and therefore hard to hit with ground fire, but also that it was both a fighter and an attack aircraft rolled into one. The only two drawbacks from an operational standpoint were the relatively light bomb load (as compared to something like the A-1 Skyraider) and the shorter range and loiter time.

The F-5 carried a liquid rain repellant system that was intended to be used only for rain removal. This consisted of a small canister of liquid in the nose landing gear area that when activated routed the liquid through tubes to spray nozzles located at the base of the windscreen. Pilots discovered that the system could also be used for removing gun and rocket contamination from the windscreen.

Phase two, the forward operating location phase, was conducted at Da Nang Air Base in northern South Vietnam. This phase took place in January of 1966. Missions flown were primarily Combat Air

Patrols (CAP). Aircraft weapons loading for these CAP flights consisted of two AIM-9B infrared heat seeking air-to-air missiles and a full load of 20mm cannon ammunition. The F-5As external wingtip fuel tanks were removed and launcher rails installed. The AIM-9B missiles were loaded on each wingtip missile launcher. The twin 20mm cannons were loaded with a total of 500 rounds of ammunition. Flight duration of between 4 ½ to 6 hours were common during this phase and were accomplished via in-flight refueling. Several missions were flown over North Vietnam during this phase.

On February 28, 1966 the Skoshi Tiger aircraft at Da Nang bombed targets in North Vietnam for the first time. Normal bomb load for air-to-ground missions in North Vietnam consisted of four 500-pound general purpose bombs, or two 750-pound general purpose bombs and the normal complement of 500-rounds of 20mm ammunition. This phase was to have lasted thirty days, however, due to a bombing moratorium imposed by then U.S. President Lyndon Johnson, the planes were directed to fly only interdiction missions on the enemy along the Ho Chi Minh Trail. This logistics pipeline for NVA operations snaked its way from North Vietnam through Laos and Cambodia ending in the southern portion of South Vietnam (in the rice rich delta area).

At the end of phase two, in February, the aircraft maintenance factor was determined to be eight maintenance man-hours per flight hour for the entire aircraft. Other USAF aircraft in operation at the time were posting maintenance factors of at least twice this figure, which means that it took more maintenance man-hours to keep these aircraft flying then the F-5.

At the end of phase two testing, all aircraft assigned to Da Nang returned to Bien Hoa air base for completion of the combat evaluation project. Phase three of the evaluation was then set to start.

Phase three, the accelerated combat sortie phase, was conducted as planned with six aircraft and would last approximately three weeks. During this phase the six aircraft flew routine combat operations supporting ground forces in war zone III, in southern South Vietnam. The aircraft, identified as red-ball aircraft because of the high turn-around times, flew approximately 24 to 30 sorties per day with 4.4 sorties per aircraft. The average was an aircraft flying five times a day supporting allied forces. Turn around times, from engine shutdown, rearm, refuel and then a thru-flight inspection averaged 20 minutes. Maintenance technicians became so proficient with the aircraft that engine changes were accomplished in less than two hours total time, including engine run-ups and checks. This was short of amazing for in-country jet aircraft of the time. The aircraft recorded a 94.5% mission accomplishment rate, with a daily operationally ready rate of 100%. Each of the six test aircraft accurately delivered an average of 12,360 pounds of ordnance on target every day of the test phase.

Phase three testing was scheduled to last until February 20th. However, on that date the test aircraft were redeployed to Da Nang Air Base in an attempt to complete the phase two testing that were cut short during the suspension of bombing imposed by President Johnson. The flight was to take place over North Vietnam. Due to the time of year, bad weather persisted over North Vietnam and the aircraft were again required to fly interdiction missions over Laos. After the end of the third week of the deployment, the weather improved and on the last day in February, the squadron started flying missions over North Vietnam. For one straight week the F-5s bombed targets and flew combat air patrols and MiG cap missions over the North. This phase of testing was completed on the 8th of March. No enemy aircraft rose to meet the Freedom Fighters during this time. With the testing completed, all aircraft returned to Bien Hoa Air Base.

On March 10, 1966 the Skoshi Tiger Combat Evaluation Program was completed and validated as a success. The squadron racked up 150 combat days totaling 2,664 combat sorties and 3116.4 combat hours. Of these, 2164 hours and 2093 sorties were flown in South Vietnam and an additional 952.4 hours with 571 sorties flown over North Vietnam, Cambodia and Laos. Six million pounds of ordnance were accurately delivered on targets. The aircraft utilization rate averaged an impressive 70 flight hours per month. (See appendix 3 for sortie generation rates). The maintenance index averaged 10 maintenance man-hours per flight hour. The results of the combat evaluation validated not only the overall aircraft's performance as a weapons platform, but also the fact that it could be maintained cost effectively by a relatively small handful of technicians.

Although one aircraft was lost, there were only eight aircraft damaged during the evaluation. The following provides a summary of those damages:

28 October 1965 - An aircraft returned from flight with a 30-caliber size hole in the top of the vertical stabilizer. The hole was assumed to have been made by a 30-caliber anti-aircraft artillery round that went completely through the vertical stabilizer. No internal damage was sustained to the substructure and the hole was patched in minimal time.

11 November 1965 - A 30-caliber hole was discovered in the intake of an aircraft during a post flight inspection. Close inspection of the aircraft revealed no damage to the engine or the aircraft substructure. A flush aluminum patch was placed over the damage and the aircraft was returned to service in minimal time.

11 November 1965 - During a post flight inspection a 30-caliber hole was found in the left hand wing tip fuel tank. Another hole was discovered in one of the 20mm cannon access door. Amazingly the wing

tip fuel tank did not explode. The gun bay was inspected and minimal damage was discovered. The aircraft was repaired in a short period of time and returned to service.

16 November 1965 - During post flight inspection a 30-caliber hole was found in the nose electronic equipment compartment access door. Necessary repairs to the door and some electronics equipment was replaced. The aircraft was returned to service in a short period of time.

1 December 1965 - Two 30-caliber holes were found during post flight inspection. One hole was discovered in the nose landing gear door and another destroyed a wing tip position light. The aircraft was repaired within one hour.

24 January 1966 - A 30-caliber size hole was discovered in the aft section of the aircraft near the engines during a post flight inspection. The damage caused more than the usual repair time, but the aircraft was made ready for the next day's missions.

4 February 1966 - A 30-caliber hole was discovered in the left aileron during a post flight inspection. The aileron was inspected, the hole routed out to ensure the repair would be long lasting and an aluminum patch was then placed over the hole. All maintenance was accomplished overnight on this aircraft and it was ready for flight the next day.

8 March 1966 - One 30-caliber size hole was discovered in the right hand wing tip fuel tank. As with the 11 November incident, the fuel tank did not explode. Repairs were accomplished overnight and the aircraft was ready for flight the next day.

The operational evaluation report summed up the Skoshi Tigers performance by stating in part:

"The F-5 is an accurate weapons delivery platform. It's maneuverability, short turn radius, and rapid response to control pressure makes it an extremely agile weapons system. In air-to-ground work, the vehicle can press closer on dive bombing, rocket firing and gun firing passes than other century series aircraft, because of its ability to "pull out" without "mushing". In addition, it is a stable platform....

(Authors note: The "century series aircraft" referred to in the above report were a series of fighter aircraft starting with the F-100 and ending with the F-110. Hence the term "100 or century series" came to be. North American Aircraft built the F-100, which was a big heavy fighter-bomber. McDonnell Aircraft built the F-101, it was a big heavy interceptor. The single seat RF-101 was used as a reconnaissance aircraft during the Vietnam war. The F-102 was a huge interceptor built by Convair Aircraft. The F-103 never made it passed the drawing boards. The F-104 was a small, light interceptor, built by Lockheed. The F-105, built by Republic Aircraft, was a huge fighter/bomber. The F-106, built by Convair Aircraft, was actually larger than its predecessor, the F-102. An F-107 was built and flown but did not progress pass the prototype stage. The F-108 and F-109 never progressed pass the drawing boards. The last of the century series fighters to be manufactured was the F-110. Secretary of Defense McNamara decided that the fighter designations needed to be standardized between the Navy and Air Force. So, in the early 1960s the F-110, which came to life as the Navy F-4B, was re-designated as the F-4C for USAF use).

Continuing with the report:

"Although no opportunity presented itself for combat evaluation in the air-to-air mode (there was practically no enemy fighter aircraft available for combat during the test), the stability of the weapons system was demonstrated dramatically while the 4503rd TFS was qualifying on the dart target during the training phase at Williams AFB, Arizona."

The glowing report also offered some recommendations on improving the performance of the aircraft. "The vehicle has excellent handling characteristics, but should have more powerful engines to increase its performance capabilities for both the air-to-air and ground roles. Heavily configured, the airplane requires a long runway for take-off (8,000 to 10,000 feet.) More elevator authority, thrust and a two-position nose strut would help in eliminating this problem." These recommendations would be taken to heart by Northrop and incorporated into the F-5E and F-5F Tiger II.

Northrop was curious as to how well the little Tigers had actually held up under combat conditions in the heat and humidity of Southeast Asia. With the concurrence of the Department of Defense, aircraft serial number 64-13317 was disassembled and flown back to Northrop for evaluation on a C-5A cargo plane. When the aircraft was opened up for inspection at the companies Hawthorn, California plant, it was discovered to be in relatively good shape. It was later returned to South Vietnam.

After completion of the combat evaluation, the eleven Skoshi Tigers remained at Bien Hoa, assigned to the USAF 3rd Tactical Fighter Wing. While a decision was awaited on turning the aircraft over to the VNAF, authorization was granted for the deployment of six additional aircraft to the squadron, bringing assigned aircraft strength to 17. One month later the 4503rd Provisional Tactical Fighter Squadron was re-designated as the 10th Fighter Commando Squadron.

The re-designated unit continued to fly direct and close air support in the II, II and IV corps areas within South Vietnam, pending squadron decommissioning and aircraft reassignment to the Republic of Vietnam Air Force. The first group of South Vietnam Air Force pilots slated to fly the F-5 as well as maintenance technicians were sent to Williams AFB in August of 1966. They would return to their homeland to fly and maintain the first supersonic aircraft assigned to their Air Force.

The following is provided as a typical tactical operation that the F-5 aircraft were involved in after the combat evaluation was complete. In March of 1967, a combined force of South Vietnamese and U.S. military personnel took part in Operation Junction City, which took place in Tay Ninh Province. The province is located approximately 60 miles northwest of Bien Hoa, near the Cambodian-South Vietnamese border. During one particularly heavy firefight, ground forces called for air support. The forward air controller in the area vectored in a flight of Skoshi Tigers to the battle. The aircraft attacked the enemy forces near Suoi Tre, a small city in the province, with 500-pound bombs, napalm and cannon fire. The successful delivery of ordnance was a key factor in the ability of allied ground forces to repel the attack. Although subjected t incessant ground fire, all aircraft safely returned to base.

Ground support missions utilized not only bomb and rockets, but also the F-5s twin 20mm M-39 cannon. The F-5A carried a total of 500 rounds of ammunition. The follow on F-5E would be designed to carry 560 rounds. The firing rate of the M-39 cannon was 1,500 rounds per minute. This rate of fire would empty the ammunition cans in 11 seconds. Muzzle velocity of the projectile was 3,250 feet per second. There were two types of 2-mm ammunition commonly used by both the USAF and VNAF in Vietnam, they were:

M56 High Explosive Incendiary (HEI) cartridge - For use in air-to-air combat was well as for light or lightly armored ground targets. It had a steel body with a thin walled casing. Weight of the composite explosive incendiary charge was approximately 0.024 pounds. When the projectile contacted the target and M505 impact fuse instantly detonated the warhead's explosive charge.

M220 Target Practice Tracer/XM242 High Explosive Incendiary Tracer - Similar to the M56 round, it had built into it an additional tracer element and two igniters. When the cartridge was fired, the burning gases would eat through an aluminum seal as the projectile traveled through the gun barrel. When the projectile departed the muzzle of the gun, the first of two charges fired and burned for approximately 15 yards. The second igniter then fired, which burned until the projectile had traveled about 75 yards. As the igniter burned out, the tracer element ignited and burned for a minimum of 1,500 yards. This allowed the pilot to actually see where the rounds were in relation to the target, and correct the air accordingly.

After firing, the shell casings were ejected overboard through a rectangular opening on the underside of the aircraft. The ammunition links were retained in the aircraft ammunition cans. Early on in the F-5 project it was discovered that if ejected overboard the links would tend to stay within the aircraft's boundary layer airflow. They would be carried by the slipstream and enter the engine intakes, damaging the engine compressor section.

Chapter 3

South Vietnamese F-5 Operations

Up through mid-1965, the VNAF consisted of a total of fourteen squadrons of two hundred and eighty-five aircraft. Of these fourteen squadrons, only four were fighter squadrons. Those four fighter squadrons were equipped primarily with the propeller driven Douglas A-1 Skyraider. This large aircraft was not a fighter, but an interdiction/attack aircraft. The VNAF fighter force was about to change with the introduction of the F-5 into the VNAF inventory.

With the success of the Skoshi Tiger combat evaluation program, the Department of Defense authorized, under the Military Assistance Program, the transfer of aircraft quantities sufficient for one squadron of F-5A and F-5B aircraft to the Republic of Vietnam Air Force. Thirty-two VNAF pilots were sent to Williams AFB for training. The first VNAF squadron identified was the 522nd Fighter Squadron assigned to the 23rd Vietnamese Fighter Wing. This transition took place on April 17, 1966. The F-5s assigned to the USAF 10th Fighter Commando Squadron were transferred to the VNAF 522nd squadron on 1 June 1967. One modification did take place before the aircraft were transferred. The in-flight refueling probes were removed as there was no need to keep them installed as the VNAF pilots had never been trained on in-flight refueling procedures. Additionally, the VNAF did not possess in-flight refueling tankers. One unspoken reason for the removal of the refueling probes and the decision not to provide tanker aircraft to the VNAF, was the concern that if allowed to, the VNAF would carry the air war into North Vietnam. The U.S. was not prepared to escalate the war to include actual offensive combat operations by the VNAF on North Vietnam. After the transfer of aircraft, the USAF 10th Fighter Commando Squadron was deactivated.

Prior to the transfer, North Vietnamese propaganda stated that the U.S. Government would never provide supersonic fighters to South Vietnam. The reason stated by the propaganda was that the U.S. did not trust the Government of the South. Consequently, the U.S. Government turning over to the VNAF the supersonic F-5 aircraft was a great boost to the moral of the South Vietnamese. Also, since the F-5 was considered a lightweight fighter with a relatively small range, the U. S. did not consider it a threat to North Vietnam and therefore not and escalation of the war. The aircraft were considered strictly a defensive weapons system.

Originally the U.S. Government was hesitant at providing the F-5 to the South because of the poor flying safety records of the VNAF. From 1962 to 1967 the VNAF had lost 287 aircraft, 153 to accidents and 134 to combat action. In 1967 alone, it had sustained 32 major accidents per 100,000 flight hours. During this same time frame the USAF had lost only 7 aircraft to major accidents. However, it should be noted that the accident figures may be somewhat skewed as the USAF had had a very successful safety program in operation for some time and also USAF pilots and ground crews were far better trained and operated better equipment then their VNAF counterparts. (See appendix 2 for loss record analysis).

Prior to transitioning to the F-5, the 522nd Fighter Squadron operated the Douglas A-1 Skyraider. In 1972 the author asked one former Vietnamese A-1 pilot how he liked flying the F-5 compared to the A-1. He stated that "It's like driving a dump truck and then getting out and driving a Cadillac!" He also stated that although the F-5 did not carry anywhere near the ordnance that the A-1 carried, it was smaller and faster and therefore harder for the enemy to hit with ground fire. The 522nd squadron's transition from the A-1 to the F-5 went off smoothly. The A-1s were retired in-place at Bien Hoa. They were parked in uncovered revetments in flyable storage. During this time frame, the

USAF held most of the aircraft parking spots at Bien Hoa and also had most of the hanger's for its own use. VNAF maintenance was accomplished in what was called the "French hanger", located at the northernmost end of the operations ramp. The French hanger was an old opened door sheet metal building that had been built by the French during their long colonial rule in Southeast Asia.

The French hanger initially housed the Grumman F8F-1 Bearcat fighters that were operated by the French Armee de l Air, and later by the Vietnamese 514th Fighter Squadron. Area wise, sufficient space was available for approximately three F-5s and two A-1s. Luckily, from a maintenance standpoint, the A-1 was built as a naval aircraft and therefore had the capability to fold its wings. This came in very handy in the cramped confines of the VNAF maintenance hangers.

The VNAF 23rd Fighter Wing had its own distinctive aircraft markings. This consisted of a very broad yellow and black checkerboard band encircling the aft section of all its aircraft. VNAF air force markings mimicked the USAF "Stars and Bars". The VNAF insignia consisted of a white star encircled by a blue background, similar to the USAF. The VNAF insignia departed from its USAF counterpart by being completely encircled in red. The "bars" consisted of a yellow background with two red bars embedded within them. A yellow and red South Vietnamese flag was painted on the vertical stabilizer. All U.S. military aircraft delivered were delivered to the VNAF under the Military Assistance Program (MAP). Legally the receiving country could not sell or transfer aircraft MAP delivered aircraft without U.S. Government approval as they were still considered U.S. Government property. This would have legal implications with MAP aircraft after the fall of the South Vietnamese Government in 1975. By the end of 1966 the U.S. Government had transferred a total of fifteen F-5s to the Government of South Vietnam through the MAP. The 522nd would remain the only

VNAF squadron operating the F-5 for about 5 years, until the Enhance and Enhance Plus Programs came to fruition.

In early 1972 the U.S. Department of Defense initiated the Enhance Programs. This was what many called a last ditch attempt to strengthen the VNAF and hasten the conversion from propeller driven aircraft to jets. Prior to enacting the Enhance Programs, the U.S. had negotiated with Iran, Taiwan and South Korea for the lease of their Freedom Fighters. As a result, one hundred and twenty-six F-5s were delivered to the South Vietnamese government in early 1973. These aircraft were disassembled and shipped to Vietnam. They were stored at Bien Hoa Air Base. The disassembly consisted of removing the wing, engines and aft section of the fuselage (commonly called the "boat tail"). The fuel tanks were defueled and purged and the ejection seats de-armed. Because of this effort, by late 1973 the VNAF was operating eight squadrons of F-5 aircraft, which comprised the F-5A, F-5B, RF-5A and F-5E models.

At the start of 1973 there were only thirty-five F-5s in the VNAF inventory. That figure would soon increase significantly. In the spring of 1973, as part of the Enhance Plus Program, eighteen brand new F-5E Tiger II aircraft arrived at Bien Hoa. These aircraft were disassembled at the Northrop facility in California and loaded onto C-5As and transported to the Philippines. In the Philippines the aircraft were reassembled by a Northrop contractor team and flown to South Vietnam by USAF pilots. The aircraft arrived with low visibility USAF markings, which were immediately replaced with those of the VNAF.

In April of 1972, the North Vietnamese Army (NVA) launched what is now called the Easter Offensive, which was an actual all out invasion of South Vietnam. The invasion hit many areas of the country. However, hit especially hard was the central region around the highland town of Kontum. At the height of the battle for Kontum in April of 1972,

VNAF fighter-bombers flew more than 150 close air support missions per day supporting ARVN ground forces. The F-5A was used extensively due to its speed and agility. F-5s carrying four 500-pound bombs devastated enemy troops and disrupted the movement of supplies to the NVA. F-5As carrying multiple 2.75-inch rocket pods unleashed a torrent of fire on enemy tanks and trucks.

Also hit hard during the invasion was the city of Quang Tri. On the 27th of April 1972, VNAF aircraft assisted the ARVN in repelling an NVA infantry assault that was backed up by Soviet supplied T-54 tanks. F-5s supplied the brunt of the intense air campaign, rocketing the tanks with their 2.75-inch folding fin air to ground rockets and pounding both tanks and infantry with 20mm cannon fire. The city changed hands several times before being taken back by the ARVN.

During the Easter invasion, VNAF units worked very closely with USAF air units, primarily in support of the Quang Tri Offensive and the battle for the town of An Loc. The South Vietnamese victory over the NVA invasion during this time should have illustrated to the American Government that the South Vietnamese military was ready to take on the NVA without the assistance of American ground troops. Unfortunately, some three years later the American Government would decide to cut off funding for the South Vietnamese in their desperate last hours.

The combined force was able to stop the invasion. The then commander of the Military Assistance Command - Vietnam (MACV), General Weyand, stated that without airpower, repulsion of the invasion would have been in doubt. One U.S. military advisor put it very bluntly when he stated that "The VNAF performed better than we had a right to expect." With only 150 fighter-bombers (A-1s, F-5s and A-37s) the VNAF flew 200 sorties per day all during the invasion. This was double the rate of the previous six months. From the 10th of March through the 28th of March, the VNAF flew almost 3,500 close air support missions and dropped a total of over 5,000 tons of ordnance.

The U.S. Government had spent a total of $753 million on the Enhanced and Enhanced Plus Programs for military equipment for the VNAF, ARVN and South Vietnamese Navy. Operation Enhance, during mid-1972, was designed to provide an infusion of much needed logistics aid that had been expended by the South during the NVA Easter Offensive of 1972. The Enhance Plus Program was an effort to increase the military stock levels to a much higher base from which the U.S. could replenish after the start of the cease fire. The terms of the cease fire would allow the U.S. Government to replace weapons on a one-for-one basis.

The rapid expansion of the F-5 inventory allowed the VNAF to stand down several A-1 Skyraider squadrons and also establish new units. The Bien Hoa F-5s were assigned to the VNAF 544th, 542nd , 540th , 536th , and 522nd squadrons. The 522nd was the original F-5 squadron, all that followed (with the exception of the 538th squadron at Da Nang) were equipped with aircraft supplied by the Enhance Plus Program. All of the Bien Hoa squadrons were assigned to the Vietnamese 1st Air Division at Da Nang. By the end of 1972, the VNAF possessed the fourth largest air force in the world. It had a total of 2,075 aircraft of 25 different types, from light observation Cessna 0-1s to the medium lift C-130 transport.

The new F-5E models delivered to the South Vietnamese incorporated many of the features recommended by the Skoshi Tiger Combat Evaluation Program. For increased take-off performance, the pilot could change the attitude of the aircraft via a switch in the cockpit. This "hike" switch controlled a two-position nose strut. When the pilot activated the switch, the nose strut would raise (hike) an additional 13-inches. This changed the attitude of the aircraft by 3.4 degrees, actually changing the wings angle of incident by 3.4 degrees. This angle change significantly reduced the aircrafts take-off roll, allowing it to become airborne in a relatively short take-off run. Once airborne, the nose strut would automatically de-hike and then be retracted into the nose wheel well for flight. The capability to raise the nose strut reduced the take-off roll by as much as one third in some cases.

The two-position nose strut had been in operation since the late 1950s with the Navy F-4B Phantom II for exactly the same reason, short take-off rolls from the deck of an aircraft carrier. Also in operation for some time was the Navy F-8 Crusader fighter which had a variable incidence wing. The wing on this aircraft could be hydraulically raised or lowered by the pilot (via a switch in the cockpit), changing the angle of incidence of the wing, thereby allowing for short take-off and landings.

Another recommendation from the Combat Evaluation incorporated into the F-5E was more powerful engines. A pair of General Electric J85-GE-13 engines each producing 4,028 pounds of thrust propelled the original F-5A/B models. The F-5Es twin J85-GE-21 engines produced 5,000 pounds of thrust each. This was a significant improvement for such a lightweight aircraft. The new engine also offered improved reliability, thus lowering the maintenance man-hours required to maintain it as well as the operating costs.

The F-5E was aerodynamically different than the "A" model. The aerodynamic refinements incorporated into the "E" allowed for an increase in speed from the F-5A maximum speed of Mach-1.4 to a maximum speed for the F-5E of Mach-1.64. The maximum ordnance load was also increased. The F-5A had a maximum external load of 5,500-pounds. The F-5E was able to carry a maximum external load of 8,000-pounds. These improvements were welcomed performance increases, which it was thought, would assist the VNAF in the prosecution of the air war. By comparison, the only other jet attack aircraft in the VNAF inventory was the Cessna A-37B Dragonfly. This aircraft had a maximum speed of 507 miles per hour, which converts to a subsonic Mach number of 0.68. The Dragonfly was also less maneuverable than the F-5 series.

The armor plating that had been added to the original Skoshi Tigers was deleted from the production F-5E aircraft delivered to the South Vietnamese. The additional 90-pounds of lead weight were deemed not a significant enough survivability item for the weight involved. Only the original Skoshi Tigers turned over to the Vietnamese after the combat evaluation were to have armor plating installed. None of the Project Enhance aircraft from other MAP countries had this armor plating installed. Interestingly, although only the original Skoshi Tigers retained the armor plating, the VNAF never elected to remove it. Apparently both maintenance and operations thought it was a good idea that should be retained at least on those aircraft carrying it. The armor plating did have two significant drawbacks. The first was, of course, a reduction in range, since the extra 90-pounds of lead weight needed to be offset by something. In the case of an aircraft, this offset was in fuel and range. The second drawback was in maintainability. Each time access was needed to components within the bays covered by the weights, they would have to be removed first, and then the access panels opened to get to the components within.

Also deleted on the F-5E were the 50-gallon wingtip fuel tanks. These tanks were installed on the F-5A/B to increase the aircraft range. They were designed to allow the aircraft to fly supersonically and as such had a distinctive "coke bottle" shape to them for supersonic flight. Wingtip missile launcher rails could be installed in place of the tip tanks. However, not generally known was the fact that the F-5A/B required either tip tanks or launcher rails installed for flight. Flying the aircraft without either installed would lead to wing damage due to harmonic oscillation during flight. The tanks or rails actually dampened the wing harmonics.

On the night of November 6th, 1972 a barrage of NVA 122mm rockets pounded Bien Hoa Air Base and surrounding communities. The rockets destroyed three VNAF F-5As parked in uncovered shelters. The author was living in a small hotel near the base and viewed this destruction from his 4th floor hotel room. The aircraft were fully loaded with fuel, 500 rounds of 20mm ammunition and each had four 500-pound general purpose bombs that had fuses installed. A 150 gallon external centerline fuel tank was also loaded on each aircraft. The resulting explosions lit up the night sky for miles around as high intensity blue flames from the exploding bombs mixed with the red flames from burning jet fuel and billowing smoke. The first light of day revealed the total destruction of the aircraft. The tritonal explosive in the bombs had cooked off due to the excessive heat of the burning aircraft. Large slabs of bomb casings were tossed hundreds of yards from the explosion site. Several rockets had landed in the town of Bien Hoa, within yards of the author's hotel. The nearby town of Tan Hep was visited by death and destruction as one unexploded rocket crashed through the roof of a house, killing a young child asleep in bed at the time.

During the latter half of 1973 an unusual occurrence took place at Bien Hoa. For several days damaged aircraft, defective aircraft parts and other miscellaneous items were brought to the south end of the F-5 operations ramp. All ramp personnel were instructed to stay clear of the area. Shortly thereafter a series of explosions went off, sending bits and pieces of components flying into the air. When asked what was taking place, one of the VNAF officers simply said that the VC had gotten onto the base and were destroying equipment. The general consensus of those that witnessed the event was that the VNAF wanted to send a message to the U.S. Congress indicating their displeasure with the funding cut backs that were taking place. The plan to blow up this equipment was actually well thought out. It was no longer of use and it could potentially send a message to Congress on the need to continue funding an ally fighting for survival. Unfortunately, the political winds had changed in the U.S., and the exhibition had no impact on future funding by the U.S. Government.

There were several unusual VNAF F-5 losses. An RF-5A loss at Da Nang in the early 1970s was the result of water contamination in the fuel system. The aircraft was loaded with three external 150-gallon fuel tanks and had just lifted off on a photo reconnaissance mission of the northern portion of South Vietnam. As it crossed the end of the runway, just after becoming airborne, both engines flamed out. Unfortunately, due to the low altitude and airspeed, the pilot had no chance of ejecting the powerless aircraft. The aircraft crashed into a large area of water just off the end of the runway. The pilot was subsequently trapped in the cockpit and drowned before rescue workers could extract him from the wreckage. An investigation team determined that a fuel truck had been contaminated by water during a recent storm. The truck serviced the aircraft the previous evening, pumping water and fuel into the fuel tanks.

Another unusual aircraft loss occurred during the summer of 1974 when an F-5A pilot, returning from a mission, decided to buzz his family home in the resort mountain town of Da Lat. Unfortunately his aircraft struck a communications tower retaining wire and crashed into a lake near the home. The right hand wingtip caught the wire, which ripped into the wing. This caused a rapid slowing and spinning of the aircraft into the lake. As in the previous case, the pilot lost his life in the crash. It should be noted that the VNAF F-5 pilots were well trained, dedicated and professional in every way. Incidents like the one just described should be considered an unusual and rare occurrence.

The ejection seats in the Vietnamese F-5s and indeed in most F-5As were what were then called the Northrop (NORAIR) standard seat. This ejection seat was really a 1950s era ejection seat that required a minimum of 50-knots airspeed and a minimum of 50-feet altitude to function properly. Some models of the F-5A/B and later F-5E/F and RF-5E were fitted with Martin Baker seats that had what was called zero-zero capability. The zero-zero capability meant that unlike the Northrop standard seats, the Martin Baker seats could successfully eject a pilot with the aircraft motionless on the ground.

In January of 1975 the VNAF lost a total of four RF-5A photoreconnaissance aircraft to ground fire. Although a stunning loss in assets, the reconnaissance package in these aircraft were not well suited for the task of photographing targets camouflaged in the jungle from 10,000 feet. The camera's in the nose of the aircraft were better suited for photographing objects out in the open such as aircraft parked on a ramp, structures in cities, etc. Weather was also a major factor impacting the quality and quantity of photoreconnaissance missions flown.

VNAF RF-5As were assigned to the 716th reconnaissance Squadron. This unit was based at Bien Hoa and fell under the auspices of the VNAF 23rd Fighter Wing. Reconnaissance pilots were drawn from the 522nd Fighter Squadron and provided the necessary training to operate the camera system as well as flight requirements. These pilots were then reattached to the 522nd and would fly photoreconnaissance missions on an as required basis. Day to day missions for these pilots would normally be to fly ground support missions from Bien Hoa assigned F-5A fighter squadrons.

The RF-5A in itself was simply a modified F-5A. The nose of the "A" was removed and the reconnaissance nose would be installed. This may seem like a simple task, but in reality it required significant expenditure of man-hours. Although removal of the standard nose was an easy and straightforward task, the reconnaissance nose installation was another matter. Not only would the hinged camera nose be installed, but also a myriad of equipment cooling air tubes, electrical wiring and cockpit controls also needed to be installed. The VNAF originally received their RF-5As already configured from Northrop. However, from 1972 to 1974 several F-5As were modified into the RF-5A configuration. Access to the cameras was straightforward. The nose was hinged at the front and to gain access to the cameras and film all that was needed was to unlock a few quick disconnect fasteners and the nose would simply swing open.

One additional benefit of the RF-5A was the fact that the camera system was accessible at shoulder height. A nominal configuration for a VNAF RF-5A flight would be three external 150-gallon fuel tanks (one on the centerline and one on each wing inboard station). Also the supersonic 50-gallon wingtip fuel tanks would normally be carried, although there were times when operating in northern South Vietnam the wingtip tanks would be removed and replaced with launcher rails having AIM-9B heat seeking missiles installed. A full compliment of 500-rounds of 20mm ammunition would also be carried for additional protection.

In January of 1975 the author traveled to Da Nang to assist the VNAF in repairing several damaged F-5s to flying status in an effort to evacuate them from the base. Da Nang was a beehive of activity during the first three months of 1975. The NVA had pushed so near the city that in March air strikes and artillery fire could be seen and heard from the base. Air strikes could be seen in the mountains surrounding the base. Columns of fire and smoke raising into the air as F-5s and A-37s carried out strikes in support of the ARVN. Four F-5Es stood air defense alert in covered shelters armed with two AIM-9B Sidewinder infrared missiles and a full load of 20mm ammunition. A centerline 175 gallon external fuel tank was installed to increase the aircrafts range. All through the war, up to March of 1975, VNAF F-5s had never been scrambled to intercept enemy aircraft attacking from the north.

Da Nang was home to the VNAF 538th Fighter Squadron. The 538th squadron was established as an F-5A squadron in early 1972. The unit assumed air defense duties from the USAF in mid-1972. Standard alert duty aircraft complement were two F-5s standing ready alert, which meant that they would be scrambled immediately. Two more F-5s were on 15 minute alert. These aircraft, in effect, were the ready alert back ups. As stated previously, the normal mission load for the alert aircraft was two AIM-9B missiles, a full load of 20mm ammunition and a centerline mounted external fuel tank.

F-5As flew ground attack and interdiction missions in support of their ARVN brethren fighting not far from the city. These missions were normally flown with four 500-pound bombs and a full load of 20mm ammunition, or two 750-pound bombs plus a full load of ammunition. Bombing runs into the mountains surrounding the area could be clearly seen from the base. The VNAF pilots expended a valiant effort, however due to funding cuts imposed by the U.S. Congress, there were just not enough serviceable aircraft or enough ordnance to make much of a difference in the final outcome. Congressional funding cuts not only impacted the VNAF, it also had a significant impact on the ARVN. Shortages of munitions and replacement parts for such critical items as cannon breaches and barrels preordained the outcome of the battles that were to take place.

Awaiting repair at Da Nang were five F-5s, two F-5Es and three F-5As. Two of the F-5As were made operational by cannibalizing parts from the aircraft deemed to have the least potential for return to flyable condition. Both F-5Es were repaired and made flyable. However one of these aircraft had a defective directional gyro. Although not a safety of flight item for such an evacuation, for some reason it was not flown out and was left for the North Vietnamese.

During the second week of March, two North Vietnamese MIG-21s over flew the base. Viewing the aircraft was quite a sight as the both completed racetrack circuits of the base, then departed heading north. The gleaming metallic silver aircraft with North Vietnamese markings was quite a sight, especially circling over an allied air base during a war. Although the alert klaxon sounded, the F-5Es on ready alert for some reason did not respond to the challenge and remained in their covered shelters. It was assumed that the MIGs were on a reconnaissance flight as the fighting had reached the mountains surrounding Da Nang.

As March near its end, it was clear that Da Nang, and indeed the northern half of South Vietnam, would soon fall into the hands of the North Vietnamese Army. The exodus of the Army of South Vietnam (ARVN) was a pitiful sight. Barges full of ARVN troops from Da Nang and the surrounding area, some Special Forces units in tiger stripped uniforms, sailed from city ports heading in a southerly direction. In town the streets were clogged with civilian refugees. By March of 1975 the city population had swelled to one million. Refugees continued to flow into the city from the surrounding countryside and from the northern reaches of South Vietnam as well as the old provincial capital of Hue. Anti-American sentiment ran high. Chants of Do Ma Ow Me (Mother F*** American) greeted us on a daily basis in town.

The base was continually hit with mortar and rocket fire. On the night prior to the last day of the authors stay, the base was hit with forty 120mm rockets. This attack destroyed quite a few structures on base as well as a brand new F-5E alert aircraft. A rocket had landed a few feet in front the fully loaded aircraft, completely destroying it. A VNAF maintenance technician standing guard duty next to it was killed.

The aircraft had accumulated less then one hundred flight hours since new. The guard, my friend, was 22 years old and being paid the equivalent of $10.00 a month by the Vietnamese Air Force.

On the 28th of March the NVA began shelling Da Nang Air Base in earnest. The VNAF 1st Air Division ordered a withdrawal of all aircraft. All serviceable F-5s and VNAF personnel were evacuated back to Bien Hoa except of course for the F-5As that could not be flown out and the F-5E that would not be flown out. Approximately 180 aircraft of various types were left for the NVA at Da Nang. This included one AC-119 gunship that had been sprayed with shrapnel by and exploding NVA 122mm rocket that the author was able to photograph. The author witnessed the World Airways evacuation of Vietnamese civilians and some military personnel from the base. Again, this was a sight to behold as scores of civilians ran towards the taxiing Boeing 727 airliners as they come towards the parking ramp. Amazingly no one was injured nor was any aircraft damaged during these ramp riots while the author was awaiting evacuation. On the 27th of March the author climbed aboard an Air America C-46 transport for evacuation back to Saigon. The aircraft was so overloaded that the author and several other men sat on the floor of the aircraft, as Vietnamese civilians and U.S. dependents occupied all the seats. Prior to departure it was noted that there were several VNAF A-37 aircraft fully loaded with bombs sitting pilot less on the taxiway at Da Nang. With canopies open, it appeared that the pilots simply gave up the fight and climbed out of the aircraft. Perhaps flying one last combat mission and then heading towards Saigon was considered too dangerous.

In late March the NVA launched an attack on the military fortifications of Ban Me Thout. Over the course of the preceding several months the NVA had moved anti-aircraft guns and surface to air missiles into South Vietnam. F-5A serial number 65-10544, tail code HJK was on a ground support mission delivering bombs on target around the city of

Ban Me Thout when the aircraft was hit by a Soviet made Strella missile. The Strella was a man-portable missile that weighed a total of 22 pounds including the weight of the launcher. The Strella was an infrared heat seeking missile that guided towards an aircrafts hot tailpipe.

As the F-5A pulled up from its bomb run, an NVA soldier on the ground raised his Strella launcher, aimed at the climbing aircraft and fired. The small missile departed the launch tube and climbed rapidly towards the aircraft. The missile flew towards the aircraft and just as it was about to enter the right hand engine exhaust it exploded. The explosion damaged the engine exhaust nozzles and sent shrapnel into the rudder and aft fuselage section. The pilot managed to keep the aircraft under control and flew back to Bien Hoa. As the aircraft settled down on the runway the landing gear collapsed due to an hydraulic system failure that prevented the gear, although appearing to be down and locked in actuality was down but not locked. During the debriefing, the pilot reported that upon pull out from the target he heard a loud bang, then the right hand engine stalled out. There were some flight control problems, but other than having an engine out, everything else remained normal throughout the flight back to Bien Hoa. The aircraft was towed to a parking spot far from the flight line and left to deteriorate. The war had progressed to the point where it was not feasible to expend manpower repairing the damaged aircraft.

A second similar incident took place in late March. F-5A serial number 65-10482 (this aircraft did not have a tail code painted on it) was also on a ground support mission, and as with the previous aircraft, was hit by a Strella and as the pilot started climbing after the bomb run the missile climbed and exploded just as it was about to enter the right hand engine tailpipe. The pilot flew the stricken aircraft back to Bien Hoa. During the debriefing the pilot reported that after he heard a loud bang he immediately experienced significant control problems. This was due to primarily to the damage inflicted on the rudder by shrapnel from the missile explosion. VNAF maintenance was so good that the aircraft was repaired and returned to service within a few days. This was truly a testament to the spirit of the Vietnamese ground support personnel that diligently crewed the aircraft.

The movement of NVA surface to air missiles and anti-aircraft weapons south forced pilots to bomb from higher altitudes, usually around 10,000 feet. This reduced the accuracy of ordnance delivery. As a result, the South lost the battle for Ban Me Thout. This victory gave the NVA a significant tactical advantage for the ultimate attack on Bien Hoa and Tan Son Nhut air bases.

The SA-7 Strella, also known with the NATO code name Grail, was accurate to an altitude of 15,000 feet. By September of 1974 the NVA had moved at least 20 anti-aircraft regiments into South Vietnam (so much for the terms of the cease fire!). These regiments were armed with the new and improved version of the Strella, which were more accurate and reliable than the old versions it replaced. Prior to the introduction of the new Strella version in 1974, the accuracy of the old SA-7 was reported to be one hit for every five missile firings. By late 1974 this had changed to a one for one average. Some of the missile hits were recorded as high as 13,000 feet. This, as can be expected, forced the VNAF aircraft to fly at an even higher altitude. This higher bombing altitude resulted in significantly reducing bomb accuracy. One drawback of the Strella was that after launch it produced a lot of smoke from the rocket exhaust. If a pilot was able to view the missile smoke trail he could out maneuver it, especially in the highly maneuverable F-5, but not so with the slow A-37.

An unusual phenomenon that VNAF F-5 pilots encountered was what was called "cockpit fog". When operating at altitudes above 10,000 feet the pilots would normally set the environmental control system (ECS) to a comfortable heat level. Once the bomb run was started and the aircraft nosed over to lose altitude and gain airspeed, the rapid loss of altitude and increase in outside air temperature created as significant temperature difference between the outside air and cockpit temperature. The result was that the cockpit would "fog up", with a condensation cloud. To counter this problem, prior to the start of the bomb run, the VNAF pilots would place the ECS control to the full hot position. The heat entering the cockpit would of course cause some discomfort to the pilot, but it eliminated the "fog".

In the early morning hours of Tuesday, April 8, 1975 a three aircraft sortie of F-5s, each loaded with four 250-pound bombs, a centerline external fuel tanks and a full load of 20mm ammunition taxied out of their covered revetments at Bien Hoa and taxied to the end of the active runway. At the end of the taxiway the aircraft pulled into the open area where the bombs were armed and the guns readied. Each then taxied onto the active runway and as all three were lined up I could hear the engines spin up in a distinctive F-5 whine. The first accelerated down the runway and as it passed the half-way point the second started its take-off roll. The first lifted off and as the second aircraft passed the runway mid-point the third and final aircraft remained behind. The pilot reported that he was experiencing engine afterburner problems. The two airborne aircraft joined up and headed towards their destination, Binh Thuan province, approximately 75 miles east of the base where NVA activity was causing havoc with the ARVN.

The third F-5 remained on the active runway for approximately five minutes and then started its take-off roll. It lifted off the runway and turned towards the capitol of the country, Saigon. This seemed a bit odd to me, but I assumed that this pilot had received instructions for a different area to attack. This would not be the case. The pilot arrived over Saigon a few minutes later and at 8:30 in the morning nosed the aircraft over and set his sights on the South Vietnamese Presidential Palace. He reached release altitude and released two of the 250-pound bombs. One bomb exploded in the palace courtyard, causing some minor damage. The second bomb was a dud and did not explode but buried itself into the palace ground.

With the two remaining bombs he started a second pass. This time both bombs detonated, but again not on the palace, but in the palace grounds. These two bombs also caused minor damage.

It is unclear as to how the pilot could have missed a direct hit on the palace itself during two bomb runs with no anti-aircraft fire directed at him. It is assumed that the agitation he felt towards the government, coupled with the nervousness he probably felt taking such action, may have impacted his judgment as to the proper release point and timing for the bomb drops. The pilot did not have the hours in the F-5 that most experienced VNAF pilots did. If this bombing run were to have been made by a more experienced VNAF pilot, the presidential palace would have been reduced to a heap of unrecognizable rubble.

One point about the utilization of the 250-pound general purpose bombs: This ordnance was seldom used by the VNAF on the F-5. The preferred bombs for use in the jungles of Southeast Asia were the 500 and 750-pounders. These ordnance had a significantly greater potential for destroying vehicles and troop concentrations that were hidden under the extensive cover of tree canopies, some of which grew to over one hundred feet tall.

After the bombing runs, the pilot then flew the aircraft over Saigon, towards the Saigon River and to the huge petroleum storage facility of Nha Be, on the outskirts of Saigon. There he emptied the entire contents of his twin 20mm cannons into the facility. Although the high explosive incendiary ammunition started several fires, they were rapidly extinguished by the facilities fire department.

It was later discovered that the pilot, 1st Lt. Nguyen Thanh Trung had defected and landed at the former VNAF air base at Phoc Long. The air base had recently been overrun and captured by NVA forces. This act provided the North Vietnamese with a fully functional F-5 and immense propaganda value. It was later determined that the pilots family lived in an area in the northern portion of the country that the government of the South had all but seceded to the North. The bombing was an act of political revenge. Lt. Trung would return to the skies of Saigon later in the month, only flying for a different country.

At the start of 1975, the VNAF had a total of 400 jet fighter and attack aircraft in its inventory. These were the F-5 fighter/bomber and the A-37 attack aircraft. All of them were in various stages of disrepair due to funding cuts by the U.S. Government. In January of 1975 the VNAF had about one-fifth of its aircraft grounded for lack of parts due to these funding cuts. This reduction in funding sealed the fate of the South Vietnamese people. By the second week of April, there were only 109 F-5s remaining serviceable in the VNAF inventory. Some of these were being flown with significant mechanical problems. Without funding, parts could not be acquired and without parts aircraft cannot fly. Without air support the war was all but lost for the South. Vietnamese maintenance technicians did their best to keep as many aircraft flyable as possible. The only method available to them was the cannibalization of parts from seriously damaged aircraft to repair others less damaged, or in need of mechanical repair. This dedication helped to keep at least some F-5s functional in the ground support role until and end of the war. In January of 1973, III corps area (the central portion of South Vietnam) was allocated 200 tactical air strikes per day. By the end of 1973, only approximately 80 air strikes were to be flown. To make matters worse, during the first half of 1974, the allocation ranged from a low of 30 to a high of 60 air strikes. This huge reduction was the direct result of the funding cuts. The strikes were not flown due to a lack of fuel, bombs and ammunition. The VNAF pilots were more than willing to fly the ground support missions, but could not without fuel and ordnance.

The final major battle of the war, as far as F-5 utilization is concerned, was the battle for Xuan Loc. This occurred during the second week of April, 1975. Xuan Loc is a large provincial city located approximately 30 miles southeast of Bien Hoa. Due to its proximity to Bien Hoa and Saigon, taking the city from the ARVN was of paramount importance to the NVA. The battle started in earnest on April the 11th in what would be called the first battle of Xuan Loc. VNAF aircraft struck enemy troop concentrations forming around the city. A total of 600 air sorties were carried out by the VNAF, many of them by F-5s flying out of Bien Hoa. The VNAF, and especially the F-5s out of Bien Hoa, provided very effective ground support to the defending ARVN ground units. The aircraft hit large troop concentrations all around the city. They also destroyed a large number of NVA vehicles. This seemed to stop the NVA push into the city.

The second battle of Xuan Loc started on April 5th, when long range enemy artillery started shelling Bien Hoa air base in an effort to keep the fighter/bombers grounded by not only destroying the aircraft, but rendering the runway unusable. This would be the first time in the war that the base would come under artillery fire. Previously the base was subjected to rocket and mortar fire. Unfortunately, because of the lack of sufficient air support as well as the lack of ammunition due to the funding cuts, the town of Xuan Loc fell to the enemy on the 22nd of the month. Due to the now precarious nature, all personnel and aircraft from Bien Hoa were evacuated to Tan Son Nhut air base, a huge facility on the outskirts of Saigon. Tan Son Nhut was also hosted the countries international airport.

During a discussion the author had during the second week of April 1975 with several VNAF F-5 maintenance technicians, one of them made an interesting comment. He stated that if the country were ever reunited, it would have quite an effective air force. When asked about the comment the technician said that the North had extensive experience in air-to-air combat because of all the air intercept and dogfight activity over North Vietnam during the American involvement. The South had extensive experience in air-to-ground operations within South Vietnam. So, combined the two would result in a very effective air force. It actually made a lot of sense.

The third week of April signaled a new chapter in the war. Captured A-37s started conducting air strikes on Saigon and its environs. The fighter/bombers, crewed by North Vietnamese pilots, flew under radar coverage on approach to Ton Son Nhut. At 5,000 feet they were spotted visually by the base air traffic control. Too late was it realized that the A-37s were flown by the enemy. They unloaded their bombs on the airfield, destroying several aircraft, including one AC-119 gunship.

The attacking aircraft were captured, fully operational, at the former VNAF base at Phan Rang located in the central section of South Vietnam. It had been reported that the flight leader of the initial attack was none other than 1st Lt. Nguyen Thanh Trung, the pilot of the F-5 that bombed the Presidential Palace in Saigon only a few weeks earlier. Although three F-5Es on alert at Tan Son Nhut were scrambled to intercept the intruders, the alert came too late and the A-37s returned to Phan Rang. The use of captured F-5s and A-37s late in the war had little military effect on the ultimate outcome, but immense impact on moral of the South Vietnamese.

On April 11th, the NVA broadcasted a report labeling all American civilian advisors in South Vietnam as soldiers of fortune. The broadcast demanded their immediate withdrawal from the country. The author departed South Vietnam on April 15, 1975. That same day Bien Hoa air base came under sustained mortar and artillery fire. Six F-5As and fourteen A-37s were damaged in the attack. Just prior to the attack, all flyable aircraft had been evacuated from Bien Hoa to Tan Son Nhut. So, as it were, the aircraft damaged during the attack were non-flyable. Continual NVA rockets and mortar bombardment rendered the base unusable.

The Cambodian airlift of food was underway during the middle of April. Five U.S. air freight carriers were contracted to supply the airborne lifeline to the Cambodian population. The primary carrier flying supplies from Saigon was the Flying Tiger Line. The carrier flew tons of rice and other supplies into the besieged Cambodian capitol of Phnom Penh. Although the freighters airlifted several thousand tons of foodstuffs into the Cambodian capitol, it was for naught. The country fell shortly after the fall of Saigon.

As The noose tightened around Saigon, F-5Es stood ready alert in hardened shelters at Tan Son Nhut, F-5, A-37 and A-1 continued to fly air strikes from the airfield, some strikes were within sight of the field. All this as an onslaught of NVA swarmed southward while the VNAF and ARVN were left fending for themselves without support from former allies. Is it any wonder why most third world countries do not trust the word of the U.S. Government.

As with the fall of Da Nang, several F-5As were abandoned on the taxiways of Tan Son Nhut during the final days of the war. It is assumed the crew decided discretion was the better part of valor and departed the country, most likely on one of the many VNAF transports that carried military personnel and dependents to a new life in exile. Continued rocket and mortar attacks destroyed a large quantity of aircraft parked in uncovered shelters on the base.

The author's flight out of the country was on an Air France 707, one of the few airlines still flying into South Vietnam. Flying to Bangkok from Saigon the author glimpsed what he thought would be the last time he would see VNAF aircraft. However, later in the month several VNAF aircraft landed on roads in Thailand, making headlines in the local papers. Interestingly, the Thai newspapers displayed photos of VNAF aircraft that had landed on narrow roads that were lined with trees. F-5s landed on roadways and deployed drag chutes that became entangled in tree limbs. On April 29th, Air Marshal Ky gave the order to his pilots to fly all operational aircraft out of the country to prevent them from falling into the enemies hands. This was probably a very wise decision, as concerns for a much wider conflict with other countries in Southeast Asia were probably on his mind. The aircraft that arrived in Thailand were loaded onto flatbed trucks and taken to local Thai air bases for final disposition. The embassy of the Republic of South Vietnam in Bangkok remained open for several months after the fall of the government that it supported.

Of those F-5s flown out of Vietnam and into Thailand, two in particular stand out. One F-5B (the two seat version) had arrived in Thailand with two pilots in each cockpit. This was accomplished by leaving the parachutes behind, lowering the ejection seat to the full down position and then having one pilot sit on the lap of the other, hunched over the top of him with his back against the canopy. This particular aircraft contained four VNAF majors. The pilots reported that they took off under rocket and mortar fire. The initial take-off was aborted when it was discovered that they had inadvertently deployed the speed brakes. This caused significant drag on the aircraft, preventing it from reaching take-off speed. Deploying the drag chute to Reduce speed on the runway, the pilot retracted the speed brakes, jettisoned the drag chute (the aircraft could not take off with the drag chute deployed) and then was able to complete the take-off while the base was still under attack. The aircraft flew onto Thailand and when it landed on the roadway the aircraft had sustained damage to the hydraulic system rendering the brakes inoperative. After landing on the narrow road, the pilot was unable to stop the aircraft and unfortunately it hit a tree at high speed, killing all four on board. This was a sad end to the valiant careers of these officers who had fought a very difficult war for their country.

One F-5A departed Tan Son Nhut amazingly with three pilots on board. This aircraft took off from the wrong end of the runway, flying over aircraft that were taxiing for take-off. The aircraft successfully flew all the way to U-Tapao Royal Thai base in southern Thailand and successfully landed on the Thai base where the aircraft was immediately impounded.

At the end of April a total of 26 VNAF F-5s (22 F-5Es and 4 F-5A/Bs) had flown out of South Vietnam and into Thailand. At least two of the single seat aircraft landed in Thailand with not only the pilot on board, but also amazingly one or more passengers sitting on the pilots lap. Many landed on local roads in various parts of the country. Others made safe landings at Thai air bases. The aircraft became a political issue in the latter part of 1975, as the now consolidated Government of the Socialist Republic of Vietnam requested the return of the aircraft. They were considered part of the countries assets. In and effort to prevent any embarrassment to the Thai government, the U.S. loaded the aircraft onto ships and transported them out of Thailand.

The logistics of transport of these aircraft is interesting. The aircraft that landed on roadways were partially disassembled and trucked to U-Tapao. Others that landed on air bases and were flyable were flown to U-Tapao. At the huge U-Tapao base, the aircraft were then loaded onto the aircraft carrier USS Midway, which then sailed onto Guam. At Guam they were offloaded. Some time later they were loaded aboard another ship and eventually ended up at McClellan Air Force Base, near Sacramento, California. There they were stored awaiting resale to allies interested in them. Many of the former battle weary fighters were turned over to the elite USAF Aggressor and USN

Top Gun squadrons for dissimilar air combat training. The small lightweight F-5s were ideal representations of the Soviet Mig-17 and -21 aircraft that were in the inventory of most third world nations that fell under the then Soviet sphere of influence. They would remain in service with these squadrons well into the twenty-first century.

The Government of the Socialist Republic of Vietnam had captured a total of 87 F-5As and F-5Bs as well as 27 F-5Es. These were incorporated into the North Vietnamese air force. They were used effectively in conducting air strikes against the Khmer Rouge forces in Kampuchea in 1978. During 1979, at least nine F-5Es, configured as air-to-air interceptors, were stationed on alert duty near Hanoi, the capitol of the now united country. These aircraft were integrated into a Mig-21 squadron, thus comprising one of the very first, and very few Warsaw Pact/NATO composite squadrons. Logistics problems forced the F-5s into extended storage. They were eventually put up for sale. Several were kept as in Vietnam as military museum pieces.

February of 1984 was an end of an era for the F-5 program as two of the original combat transitioning training aircraft were retired from USAF service. The 425th Tactical Fighter Training Squadron at Williams AFB in Arizona held ceremonies retiring F-5B serial numbers 64-1033 and 64-1408. These two aircraft were originally assigned to the 4441st Combat Training Squadron, which had been formed in the 1960s to train foreign pilots and maintenance technicians, many of them Vietnamese, on the F-5 series aircraft.

Chapter 4

A Day in the life of a VNAF F-5 Pilot

VNAF F-5 pilots continually placed themselves in harms way defending their country. The following is provided as a typical sortie carried out by an F-5E Tiger II pilot during April of 1975. It must be understood that combat missions flown all during the Vietnam War were extremely hazardous to all allied pilots, regardless of the type of aircraft they were flying. However, the VNAF pilots were subjected to horrendous hazards late in the war.

The 522nd Fighter Squadrons operations building was located on the south end of the flight ramp near the Bien Hoa air terminal. Pilots would report to the operations building prior to flight for a mission briefing that covered the location of the air strike and the ARVN ground unit's the flight was supporting. Also covered was what to expect as far as anti-aircraft fire was concerned. The location of both friendly and enemy forces were covered in detail. Call signs were issued and radio frequencies identified for both air and ground use. Forward Air Controllers (FACs) were also identified as to aircraft type, altitude and radio frequency. Once the briefing was complete, the pilots would generally be driven out to their assigned aircraft.

At the aircraft the pilot would receive a briefing from the aircrafts crew chief. The briefing covered the status of the aircraft, any maintenance issues on the aircraft that would be of concern (remember in April funding for the war was cut off by the U.S. Government. This resulted in aircraft that were being flown with maintenance issues). Once satisfied with the aircrafts condition, the pilot would conduct a preflight inspection, walking around the aircraft to ensure to his satisfaction that all appeared to be in order, at least from a visual standpoint is concerned. While conducting the walk-around inspection the pilot was clad in standard Nomex flight suit as well as an anti-g suit.

The heat and humidity of the Bien Hoa climate would create such profuse preparation that by the time the inspection was complete, his flight suit would be drenched in sweat. Of paramount importance during the walk-around inspection would be the condition of the ordnance, the fuse settings and the correct arming wire routing. Rocket pods, if installed, required particular attention. As many as twenty-four 2.75-inch folding fin rockets could be loaded into each pod. Each rocket needed to be inspected to ensure that it was properly loaded and all electrical connection made. The gun bay doors would be opened by the crew chief prior to pilot's arrival. The pilot would check to ensure the gun was loaded and all electrical connections made. After inspection of the gun, the crew chief would close and secure the gun bay access panels. Once the inspection was complete the pilot would don his parachute and climb into the cockpit. VNAF F-5E aircraft did not have the Martin Baker ejection seats. The Martin Baker seats incorporated a pilot's parachute into the upper portion of the seat. As such, the pilot only needed to put on a parachute harness and once seated in the cockpit, he would then hook up to the seat/parachute assembly.

Engine start and taxi would be typical, however due to the continual rocket and mortar attacks, the pilot would, at times, need to taxi clear of craters caused by exploded enemy missiles. Once clear of these obstacles, and at the end of the active runway, the aircraft would be stopped by a munitions crew chief. The end of runway munitions crews would arm the weapons prior to take-off. A final aircraft inspection was also accomplished to ensure that nothing was leaking from the aircraft. A thumbs up signal from the munitions crew chief would allow the pilot to take the active runway when cleared to by the control tower. During the taxi and end of runway checks, the engines would be at or near idle settings, which meant that there would be very little cooling air flowing into the cockpit from the aircrafts air conditioning system.

Once cleared to take the active runway, the pilot activated the nose strut extension switch and the nose landing gear shock strut extended some 13-inchs raising the nose of the aircraft up considerably. An F-5E loaded with four 500-pound bombs, a full 175-gallon centerline fuel tank, a full load of 20mm ammunition as well as a full internal fuel load of JP-4 would require a take-off run of approximately 5,800 feet before lift-off. However, with the 10,000 foot runway at Bien Hoa such a take-off run was no problem. By comparison, a similarly loaded F-5A would require approximately 7,800 feet of runway to take-off.

Climbing out the aircraft could be subjected to small arms fire, and during cruise to the target area the aircraft would be subjected to anti-aircraft fire from both 30-mm optically tracked cannon and man-portable Strella missiles. The NVA had also moved radar-controlled SA-2 surface-to-air missiles into the South and started to ring the area with these deadly missiles. Both the SA-2 and Strella man-portable missiles presented a very real threat to the pilot, but if visually detected in time, could be outmaneuvered by the nimble F-5E. Normal cruise time to a target area in April of 1975 was measured in minutes, as enemy forces were continually advancing south towards the capital.

As the pilot neared the target area, a VNAF Forward Air Controller (if not already shot down, which was an unfortunate increasingly common occurrence during the closing months of the war) would direct the pilot to a specific target, troop concentration, vehicles, etc. If no FAC were available, and communications could not be established with the ground controller, the pilot would take it upon himself to select targets on a priority basis. All during this time the pilot would be subject to intense ground fire.

One can imagine the pilot pushing the control stick forward, nosing the aircraft over at the start of the bomb run and seeing the windscreen fill with red-hot steel lifting up and passing over and under the aircraft as NVA gunners attempted to track and shoot down the incoming aircraft. Tracer rounds from 30-mm cannons, 50-caliber machine gun fire and small arms fire all directed, at what seemed to the pilot right at his head, would seem to fill the windscreen. Although bombing from 10,000 feet was considered the safe and smart thing to do, VNAF pilots were just as dedicated to supporting their brethren on the ground as their USAF, USN and USMC counterparts. And so, most air strikes took place well below this altitude, regardless of the consequences. In this environment, the small size, maneuverability and speed of the F-5 was a plus in survivability.

Weapons release and climb out subjected the pilot to the threat of the deadly Strella missile. During climb out the pilot would continually scan rearward, craning his neck back left and right as much as possible to "check six" for possible missile launches, all the while still subjected to significant amounts of small and medium caliber ground fire. Should the aircraft sustain a hit or hits significant enough to render the aircraft uncontrollable, requiring the pilot to eject from the crippled jet, then unlike his American military counterparts, he would not be the subject of a massive rescue operation. Instead VNAF pilots were left to their own skills in eluding the enemy and hopefully making their way back to friendly comrades or home base. If captured, they would not be escorted to a prisoner of war camp and used as a bargaining chip. They would normally be subjected to an intensive intelligence sessions by the enemy attempting to extract as much information as possible and then the pilot would more than likely face summary execution.

Should the pilot be lucky enough to make it back to Bien Hoa, he would only have to look forward to repeating a very similar mission anywhere from one to several hours later depending on his condition. VNAF pilots were subjected to hardships unlike anything experienced by their American military counterparts. They were dedicated to supporting the ARVA units and did so until the very end of the war. The

F-5 carried a significant burden flying both combat air patrols and ground support missions. It was the only modern aircraft in the VNAF inventory to do so.

Chapter 5

Combat Effectiveness Summation

How effective were the Northrop F-5s in Vietnam?

Starting in early 1972, the F-5 assumed all air defense duties for South Vietnam. Prior to 1972, the USAF provided air defense duties, initially with the F-102 Delta Dart, and later with the F-4 Phantom II. Air defense was a significant responsibility for any aircraft, in both war and peace. The F-5 was the only aircraft capable of fulfilling this role, and although the North Vietnamese air force conducted no air strikes in the South during the war (disregarding strikes conducted by captured VNAF aircraft at the very end of the war), the threat was real. During the Skoshi Tiger Combat Evaluation, F-5As operated by the USAF conducted air patrols over North Vietnam. No enemy aircraft were encountered during these combat air patrols. Later, the USAF Fighter Weapons School and the USN Top Gun School would use the F-5 series as a dissimilar air combat aircraft, simulating a variety of Soviet aircraft. Tactics and training provided by the F-5 would become valuable tools to both America and her allies. After the fall of South Vietnam, F-5Es remaining in Vietnam were reported to have been incorporated into the unified Vietnamese air force and placed on ready alert in the Hanoi area.

The RF-5A was the only supersonic jet photoreconnaissance aircraft in the South Vietnamese air force inventory. Although the cameras in the nose of the aircraft were not designed for photographic work in the jungles of Southeast Asia, the reconnaissance imagery provided by the aircraft was significant in assisting the South Vietnamese in the prosecution of the war, especially during 1974-75. The cameras in the aircraft were able to detect troop and vehicle movements just prior to the enemy initiating all out offensives. Without the capabilities of the RF-5As several battles during these years could have resulted in the NVA overrunning key areas sooner.

All VNAF versions of the F-5 (A/B/E and even the RF-5A) were also assigned to the fighter-bomber role supplementing the A-37, and late in the war the A-1. By comparison, the A-37B had a maximum external ordnance load of 5,400 pounds. The F-5A and F-5B had a maximum external load of 6,200 pounds. The F-5Es maximum load was 8,000 pounds. So, as can be seen, the F-5 series could deliver more ordnance on target than the A-37B. One other difference between the F-5 and A-37 was range. The A-37 had an edge in range with maximum payload, which was listed as 460 miles. The F-5As maximum payload range was 220 miles, and the F-5Es maximum payload range was 200 miles. Range during the last days of the war was not an issue, as most air strikes were taking place within a very short distance from most VNAF bases that were still in commission.

The F-5s were the only supersonic fighter-bombers in the VNAF inventory. The supersonic speed and small size of the aircraft made it extremely difficult for NVA gunners to hit until late in the war when significant numbers of anti-aircraft weapons had rolled into South Vietnam, many of which were radar controlled. The F-5A was also one of the very few VNAF aircraft to conduct air strikes into North Vietnam. During the USAF combat evaluation program, F-5As operated by the USAF in South Vietnam also conducted air strikes in the southern portion of North Vietnam.

Lastly, the F-5 provided a much needed boost to the moral of not only the VNAF, but also the South Vietnamese population in general. Providing supersonic jet aircraft to the South sent a clear message of American intent to provide the people of South Vietnam with a significant airborne capability to defend themselves with.

Although it is difficult to determine, had the U.S. Congress provided the required financial aid that was initially authorized for the 1974-75 fiscal year, the outcome of the 1975 NVA offensive could have potentially been much different. The significant reduction of air strikes reported in the previous chapter of this book were a direct result of the funding cuts. As previously stated, both the VNAF and ARVN were seriously crippled in their efforts to support and prosecute the war by these cuts. Vietnamization was taking hold in the military. The morale of the civilian populace, as well as the military, concerning Vietnamization was initially one of reticence. However, in the early 1970s the morale had improved considerably. Both the military and the civilian population came to realize that they had a very real chance of settling the conflict through negotiations. This, of course, could only be accomplished with a strong South Vietnamese military that was financially and logistically supported by the U.S.

Vietnam would not be the end of combat for the F-5. A scant decade and a half later, Northrop Tigers would again be called into service to enter combat, this time over the skies of the Middle East during Operation Desert Storm. RF-5As and F-5Es would fly reconnaissance missions for the coalition air forces. F-5E and F-5F Tiger II aircraft, flown by Saudi pilots, would fly combat air patrols, as well as air-to-ground support missions during the conflict. The Bahrain Air Force would also provide F-5Es and F-5Fs in support of the coalition air forces. The improved Tiger II of these Middle Eastern countries carried with them the knowledge gained from the Skoshi Tiger program decades earlier.

Photo Pages

Photo 1 - VNAF F-5A assigned to the 522nd Fighter Squadron at Bien Hoa Air Base was photographed on the flight ramp in 1973. Yellow and black checkerboard band around the aft fuselage are the colors of the 23rd Tactical Wing. Tail codes, in this case "HBA" were not painted on all aircraft. Supersonic wingtip fuel tanks with their distinctive "coke bottle" shape is clearly visible on the right hand wing tip of this aircraft. On the F-5E and F-5F these tanks were deleted. The tip tanks could be easily removed and AIM-9B missile launcher rails installed. Centerline 150-gallon fuel tank has been installed. Covered aircraft shelters are visible in the background.

hoto 2 - F-5B serial number 65-10586 taxies out of its covered shelter at Bien Hoa with an air gunnery target (dart) under the left wing. The tow target operator sits in the aft cockpit. The "dart' was used to train new F-5 pilots in the art of air-to-air combat. Once in the practice area the tow operator would release the dart and a long steel cable would keep the object suspended far behind the tow aircraft. Multiple passes could be made by attacking F-5s. Colored rounds would indicate which hits came from what aircraft. At the end of the training period, the tow operator would release the dart, which would then free fall back to earth. It would be recovered by a ground crew and returned to the base for hit analysis. This was just one of many roles the F-5B provided for the VNAF. Covered aircraft shelters at Bien Hoa are clearly viewed in this photo. The shelters had reinforced concrete over thick steel half domes.

Photo 3 - View of the Bien Hoa F-5 parking ramp circa 1974. As can be seen in the photo, the ramp had a mix of covered and uncovered shelters. Aircraft in foreground is an F-5A that had been delivered to the VNAF from other MAP country air force. A close look at the photo will reveal supersonic wing tip tanks that are camouflaged and obviously were not originally part of this particular aircraft. Visible between the two engines, at the base of the vertical stabilizer is the open drag chute door. The drag chute was used to decelerate the aircraft after landing, however because of the long runway at Bien Hoa the drag chute was rarely used.

Photo 4 - An F-5A loaded with a typical ground support ordnance load, consisting of four 500-pound general purpose bombs, a 150-gallon centerline fuel tank and a full load of 20mm ammunition. The photo shows the bombs with fuse extenders installed. When the bomb fuses (located at the tip of the extender tube) contacted the ground they would set the bomb off, thus exploding it slightly above the ground causing greater lateral damage than a bomb without extenders installed. Small fuse propellers are visible on the end of the fuse. An arming wire retaining clamp is also visible encircling the fuse extender tube near its mid-point (dark line on tube). Arming wires are also visible running from the fuse propeller to the aft section of the bomb. Open triangular access door on the aft section of the fuselage in this photo is the engine oil filler cap and dip stick access. Yellow coloring around the bomb indicates it is a general purpose, tritonal filled ordnance.

Photo 5 - An F-5A in a covered shelter at Bien Hoa circa late 1973. Aircraft is loaded with two 750-pound general purpose bombs installed on the inboard station of both wing pylons. Note the white leading edge of the vertical stabilizer. The leading edge of the vertical stabilizer was damaged by ground fire and replace, but not painted to match the camouflage paint of the aircraft. A new right hand main landing gear tire is clearly visible in the photo. The F-5 series was very good with tire wear, since it landed at a very light weight and braking was not an issue. Centerline 150-gallon external fuel tank is visible loaded on the pylon under the aircraft. Northrop standard ejection seat headrest is visible in the cockpit.

Photo 6 - A view of a 750-pound bomb loaded on the inboard pylon of an F-5A parked in an open, uncovered shelter at Bien Hoa. Visible across the aircraft is an F-5A in a covered shelter. Photo was taken in late 1973.

Photo 7 - January 1975, two F-5As at Bien Hoa are being readied for air defense duties at Da Nang. Wingtip fuel tanks (seen on ground between the two aircraft) have been removed and replaced with missile launcher rails. AIM-9B missiles have been loaded on the launcher rails. Both aircraft have centerline installed 150-gallon fuel tanks. Although the F-5E was standing ready alert at Da Nang at the time, these two F-5As were dispatched to support them. Photo illustrates the paint differences that existed with the VNAF F-5s. Aircraft on the left in the photo was one of the original F-5As delivered to the VNAF. Aircraft on the right in the photo was a MAP country aircraft delivered later in the war. Yellow vehicle under the left aircraft is a bomb loader. Yellow engine start cart used to provide compressed air to start the engines is visible between the aircraft. VNAF maintenance technicians worked very hard to support the war effort.

Photo 8 - An F-5A parked on the flight ramp at Bien Hoa in late 1974. This aircraft was configured as an air defense aircraft and was being readied to stand interceptor duties at Bien Hoa. Late in the war the F-5As five minute air defense alert in covered shelters at the end of the runway, similar to those at Da Nang. AIM-9B missile is visible on the right hand wingtip missile launcher. Unpainted 150-gallon centerline fuel tank is visible and contrasts sharply with the camouflaged aircraft. Dark rectangular object hanging from under the aft section of the aircraft is an open engine start access door.

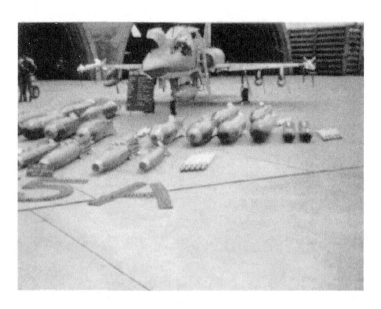

Photo 9 - Taken at Bien Hoa in mid-1974, this is a static display of F-5A weaponry. A rare event during the war, the display was exhibited for visiting South Vietnamese Air Force staff members. Photo shows the open gun access doors on the forward section of the fuselage, forward of the cockpit. AIM-9B missiles are loaded on the wingtip missile launcher rails. A centerline 150-gallon fuel tank is also visible. Four general purpose 500-pound bombs are loaded on the under-wing stations. Visible in the foreground are the wide variety of ordnance the aircraft could carry. Visible are 250, 500 and 750-pound bombs. Also visible on the ground in the center of the photo are 2.75-inch folding fin unguided rockets that were carried in pods. Largest pod carried contained 24 of these rockets. Foreground, spelling out F-5A, are rounds of 20mm cannon ammunition. The F-5A carried 500 rounds of ammunition. Bombs do not have fuses installed for safety.

Photo 10 - Same display day, but photo shows and F-5E on display. Note the bombs on the ground just behind the F-5E that is spelled out on the ground with the 20mm ammunition The two bombs at the end of each forward row contain deceleration devices. Upon release from the aircraft, these small rectangular pads open up to slow the bombs speed. This allows the aircraft to release the bomb from extremely low altitude and consequently not be damaged itself by the explosion. The canisters with the black dots on them at of the middle row are pods that house the 2.75-inch folding fin rockets (rockets are not visible in this photo). Canisters at the end of this row, with multiple holes visible are rocket pods with the covers removed. Also partially visible in the extreme left of the photo is a target tow dart used to train pilots in air gunnery. Bombs do not have fuses installed for safety.

Photo 11 -F-5As undergoing maintenance in the "French Hanger" at Bien Hoa in 1973. During the American involvement, the F-5s were regulated to such hangers for maintenance. This continued after the departure of the USAF, as the facility was furnished to support the F-5 and moving everything made no sense. As can be seen, the hanger was simply a sheet metal, open air building with no doors to protect the aircraft during storms. As can be seen, because of its small size, up to eight F-5s could fit in the hanger. Only two USAF F-4 Phantom IIs would fit in the hanger.

Photo 12 - A-1 Skyraiders undergoing maintenance at Bien Hoa late in the war. These aircraft were placed in storage for a time because of the influx of F-5s and A-37 jets. It was felt that the slow Skyraider was vulnerable to small arms ground fire and as such it was replaced with the newer, faster jets. However, late in the war these valuable craft were brought back into service in an effort to stave off the advancing NVA. The Skyraider could carry a significant ordnance load. The VNAF operated various models of the aircraft, as can be seen in the photo. Aircraft in the foreground has had its engine and folding wing sections removed. VNAF maintenance technicians cannibalized parts from aircraft to get as many flyable as possible. The fact that the aircraft was old and parts were difficult to come by coupled with the funding cuts by the American government made maintenance on these craft very difficult, requiring ingenuity on the part of the VNAF.

Photo 13 - The remains of a Da Nang based F-5E destroyed by an NVA 122mm rocket that landed just in front of the aircraft, which was at the time parked in a covered shelter. The "lucky" hit destroyed the aircraft and killed the 22 year old crew chief standing guard at the time. Complete destruction of the aircraft is evident in the photo. Angled half tube in the aft of the shelter are blast deflectors that directed the aircraft engines exhaust up and out of the shelter during engine runs.

Photo 14 - Authors "ride" to and from Da Nang was aboard an Air America C-46 transport. Photo shows the C-46 that delivered the author to Da Nang shortly after landing. Air American operated a wide selection of aircraft in Southeast Asia, and contrary to popular belief, acted as a humanitarian airline supplying local Southeast Asia villages with foodstuffs and other items. Of course, it also supported the war effort. Most popular movies and literature about Air America are pure fiction, however the brave pilots of Air America performed some very heroic feats.

Photo 15 - Da Nang, March 1975. An F-5E alert aircraft is scrambled on a practice air intercept mission. These practice alerts were conducted on a routine basis to rotate the aircraft in and out of alert status. The same procedure was used by USAF aircraft based all over the world. The view shows the F-5E taxiing with the nose strut in the "de-hiked" position. Alert pilots would start and taxi the aircraft clear of the shelters with the strut de-hiked". They would "hike" the strut during their taxi to the active runway. Alert shelters are visible as the half-dome structures in the background. The alert shelters at Da Nang originally housed USAF F-4 Phantom II interceptors.

Photo 16 - Same Da Nang alert aircraft. Photo was taken seconds after photo 15 and now shows that the nose landing gear strut has been "hiked". Comparing photo 15 with photo 16, the significant change in the angle of the nose is clearly evident. The "hike" feature allowed the F-5E and F-5F to take-off in a shorter distance than a similarly loaded F-5A or F-5B. The incorporation of this feature was a direct result of the recommendations made after the F-5A combat evaluation program of the original USAF F-5A Skoshi Tiger aircraft. White wingtip AIM-9B and centerline 175-gallon fuel tank are clearly visible in the photo.

Photo 17 - An RF-5A on the flight ramp at Bien Hoa, late 1974. This aircraft had recently been cleaned, serviced and readied for a photoreconnaissance mission. Three external 150-gallon fuel tanks are loaded. Nose camera windows are clearly visible in the photo. The only difference between the F-5A and the RF-5A was the installation of the reconnaissance nose, painted black in the photo. Internally, additional wiring and coolant air tubes were installed that were not part of the F-5A. The change was accomplished via a package that contained everything needed for the conversion. This particular aircraft was converted by the VNAF at Bien Hoa, hence the unpainted nose. Yellow tow bar is attached to the nose landing gear strut for aircraft movement on the ground.

Photo 18 - The evacuation of Da Nang, March 1975. Difficult to see in the photo is a World Airways 727 that is taxiing in to the Da Nang airport terminal. Hoards of frightened Vietnamese civilians swamped the aircraft.

Photo 19 - F-5A serial number 65-10482 returned to Bien Hoa after a ground support mission after being hit by a shoulder launched heat seeking missile. The missile exploded prematurely just as it was about to enter the right hand engine exhaust. The pilot heard a loud bang and felt a jolt to the aircraft. As can be seen in the photo, the engine exhaust nozzles were completely destroyed and the aft section of the fuselage peppered with shrapnel holes.

Photo 20 - The pilot of aircraft 10482, seen in photo, discusses the mission with the author and ground crew shortly after parking the aircraft. The aircraft was returned to operational service within a few days, which is a testament to the dedication of the VNAF maintenance technicians.

Photo 21 - F-5A serial number 65-10544 also sustained a ground to air infrared missile hit after pull out from a bombing run. The missile exploded just as it entered the engine tailpipe blowing the engine nozzles off the aircraft and significantly damaging the aft section of the fuselage as well as the right hand horizontal stabilizer and rudder. The hit damaged the utility hydraulic system and as a result, although the landing gear extended, it failed to lock. The landing gear collapsed on landing. The pilot stated that after the loud bang, the aircraft shook and became uncontrollable. He was able to stabilize the aircraft and flew it back to home base at Bien Hoa. Note the holes in the rudder and the significant damage to the right hand engine area. Because this occurred so late in the war (1975) it was decided that it should not be repaired.

Photo 22 - Close-up view of the damaged right hand engine exhaust of aircraft 65-1054. The collapsed right hand landing gear is visible under the horizontal stabilizer in the bottom right hand section of the photo. Aircraft jacks are just visible in the lower right and left hand portions of the photo. Left hand fuselage aft section jack is visible as the yellow object in the lower left hand of the photo. Aircraft remained on jacks until the fall of Bien Hoa when it was completely destroyed in a rocket and mortar attack.

Photo 23 – A very young author at Bien Hoa Air Base, April 1975. Flak jacket's were issued and worn. F-5A in uncovered shelter had just returned from a ground support mission. Open door just above the engine housed the drag chute. This aircraft used the drag chute upon landing. After landing drag chutes were jettisoned after turning off of the active runway. They were then picked up by a ground crew and returned to the parachute shop to be inspected and repacked for further use.

Photo 24 – The remains of an RF-5A that crashed off the end of the runway at Da Nang. Water contamination in the fuel caused both engines to flameout. The pilot died in the crash. As can be seen, the canopy frame is still attached to the aircraft indicating the pilot did not attempt to eject from the stricken craft.

Photo 25 – Flight line maintenance, Bien Hoa circa mid-1974. One unique feature of the T-38/F-5 series was the ability to raise the windscreen allowing access to the back side of the instrument panel. Aircraft being worked on is an F-5A. Note the F-5A also undergoing maintenance parked next to it. An A-1 Skyraider can be seen in the background as well as a UH-1 Huey helicopter.

Photo 26 – Enhance Project F-5A being delivered to the VNAF at Bien Hoa. Aircraft is from Iran as can be seen by the desert paint scheme. Due to the vast influx of aircraft into the South Vietnamese Air Force inventory during the Enhance and Enhance Plus Program, the VNAF did not have the manpower, nor the time to re-paint the aircraft. In all, 126 F-5s were delivered to the VNAF during the Enhance Programs. A total of 126 F-5s were delivered. Theses aircraft came from the inventories of Iran, Taiwan and Korea. All F-5 series aircraft were easily disassembled for shipment. Preparatory work included defueling and de-arming the ejection seat. Disassembly consisted of removing the wing and aft fuselage section.

(USAF photo)

Photo 27 – A flight of three F-5Es at the end of runway check area at Bien Hoa. Aircraft are preparing for a check flight and are undergoing final inspection by VNAF ground maintenance crews to ensure that the aircraft are ready for flight. All three aircraft have had their nose strut "hiked" in preparation for flight. The aircraft are clean, with no external stores except for the centerline pylon.

Photo 28 – Rocket attack on Bien Hoa, September 1974. Starting in late 1974, the NVA launched steadily increasing attacks on installations in South Vietnam. Soviet and Chinese supplied rockets rained death and destruction upon civilian and military alike.

Photo 29 – Unique view of the Bien Hoa flight ramp taken September 1974. Photo was taken looking over the left hand wing of a VNAF RF-5A. Supersonic wingtip fuel tank is visible in the lower left hand of the photo. Reconnaissance nose is visible in the right hand section of the photo. Landing is an Air America UH-1 contracted to the ICCS, the International Committee for Controls and Supervision. The ICCS members did very little to monitor the agreed upon cease fire.

Photo 30 – VNAF F-5A immediately after landing at U-Tapao Royal Thai Air Base in southern Thailand. USAF maintenance technicians scramble around aircraft to ensure that the guns are not loaded and armed. VNAF pilot and additional passenger can be seen ready to climb out of the cockpit. Such events were not unusual with VNAF aircraft landing in Thailand.

(USAF photo)

Photo 31 – A VNAF F-5E is seen being loaded onto the deck of the aircraft carrier USS Midway stationed in the Gulf of Thailand in May of 1975. The aircraft landed on a Royal Thai Air Base and is being airlifted by a USAF CH-53 heavy lift helicopter. The F-5 was a relatively light load for the heavy lifter. This particular F-5E was apparently configured for air defense as it does not have any wing mounted weapons pylons installed.

(USN Photo)

Photo 32 – USAF Skoshi Tigers Vietnam bound. A flight of the original USAF F-5A Skoshi Tigers being refueled over the Pacific Ocean by a KC-135A refueling tanker . As can be seen in the photo, the Skoshi Tigers were equipped with an in-flight refueling probe mounted on the left hand side of the fuselage. The refueling probes were removed when the aircraft were handed over to the VNAF after the Combat Evaluation of the aircraft was completed. Each of the aircraft in the photo carries a centerline mounted 150 gallon fuel tank. Supersonic wing tip fuel tanks can also be seen mounted at each wingtip. The F-5A and F-5B were capable of carrying a total of three 150 gallon external fuel tanks.

(USAF photo)

Appendix 1

Skoshi Tiger Combat Evaluation Serial Numbers

The following is a complete listing of all USAF F-5A aircraft assigned to the Skoshi Tiger Combat Evaluation Program at Bien Hoa Air Base, South Vietnam as well as the date the aircraft were assigned to the USAF 4503rd Tactical Fighter Squadron:

Serial Number	Date Assigned	Comments
63-8424 Program Aircraft	08 October 1965	Original Sparrow Hawk
63-8425	30 September 1965	
63-8426 Program Aircraft	11 October 1965	Original Sparrow Hawk
63-8428 Program Aircraft	05 October 1965	Original Sparrow Hawk
63-8429 Program Aircraft	06 October 1965	Original Sparrow Hawk
64-13314 Program Aircraft	11 October 1965	Original Sparrow Hawk
64-13315	23 September 1965	
64-13316	17 September 1965	
64-13317	22 September 1965	

64-13318	24 September 1965
64-13319	27 September 1965
64-13332	28 September 1965

Appendix 2

USAF Aircraft Loss Record Reference

Calendar Year 1965 USAF Aircraft Losses

Type	F-5	F-100	F-4
Combat	1	14	2
Operational	0	0	0

Calendar Year 1966 USAF Aircraft Losses

Combat	0	20	4
Operational	0	0	3

Calendar Year 1967 USAF Aircraft Losses

Combat	0*	28	15
Operational	0*	15	0

*Note: The Combat Evaluation Program was completed near the end of 1966. The combat loss record for 1967 is provided as a reference to the other USAF aircraft losses as the war in Vietnam gradually escalated.

Appendix 3

Skoshi Tiger Sortie Generation Rates

1965	Sorties	1966	Sorties
October	155		
November	719		
December	643		

1966	Sorties	1966	Sorties
January	421	July	457
February	595	August	390
March	413	September	451
April	267	October	614
May	353	November	805
June	367	December	708

1967	Sorties
January	727
February	595
March	767
April	Aircraft Transferred to VNAF

Average Sortie Generation Comparison for 1966

Aircraft	Sortie Rate
F-5	1.31
F-100	1.00
F-4C	0.84

Appendix 4

F-5A/E Specifications

Overall Dimensions Configuration	F-5A (MAP Configuration	F-5E (Standard
Length	47 ft. 2 in.	47 ft. 4.8 in.
Height	13 ft. 2 in.	13 ft. 4.2 in.
Wingspan	25 ft. 3 in.	28 ft. 8 in.
Wing Area	169.98 sq. ft.	195.68 sq. ft.
Gross Weight	20,677 lbs.	24,722 lbs.
Propulsion		
Engine Type	J85-GE-13	J85-GE-21
Thrust (Maximum) engine)	4,028 lbs. (per engine)	5,000 lbs. (per
Performance		
Max. Level Flight	Mach 1.40	Mach 1.64
Combat Ceiling	50,000 ft.	51,200 ft.
Maximum Range miles	1,375 Nautical miles	1,515 Nautical
Rate of Climb ft./minute	28,700 ft./minute	34,300

Maximum Payload	6,200 lbs.	8,000 lbs.
Radar	None	AN?APQ-159

F-5A

Freedom Fighter

Standard Military Assistance Program (MAP) Configuration

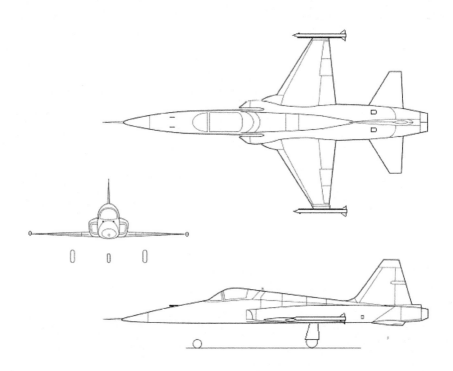

F-5C

Vietnam Configuration

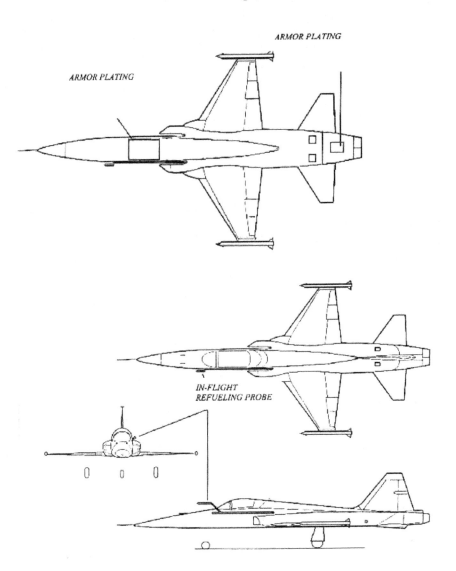

ARMOR PLATING

ARMOR PLATING

ARMOR PLATING

IN-FLIGHT
REFUELING PROBE

RF-5A

Standard Vietnam Configuration

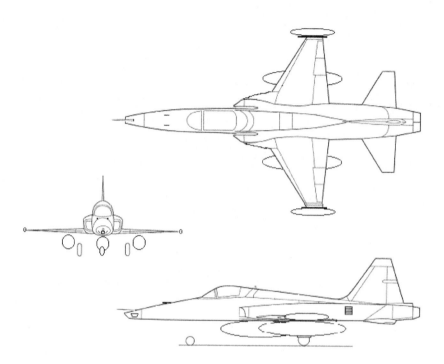

F-5A

External Stores Loading

Vietnam Configuration

Stores Type	Tip	Outboard	Inboard	Centerline	Inboard	Outboard	Tip
50 Gal. Fuel Tank	*						*
150 Gal. Fuel Tank			*	*	*		
275 Gal. Fuel Tank			*		*		
Aim-9 Missile	*						*
MK-36 500 lb. Bomb		*	*	*	*	*	
MK-82 500 lb. Bomb		*	*	*	*	*	
M-117 750 lb. Bomb		*	*	*	*		
MK-83 1000 lb. Bomb			*	*	*	*	
MK-84 2000 lb. Bomb				*			
BLU Fire Bombs		*	*	*	*	*	
CBU Cluster Bombs		*	*	*	*	*	
2.75 in. 7 Rocket Pod		*	*		*	*	
2.75 in. 19 Rocket Pod		*	*		*	*	
LAU-10/A 5 in. Rockets		**	***	***	**		
SUU-20 Bomb/Rocket Pack				*			
SUU-25 Flare Pod		*				*	
6 Each Mk-82 Bomb Pod				******			
3 Each MK-82 Bomb Pod			***	***	***		

F-5E

(Vietnam Configuration)

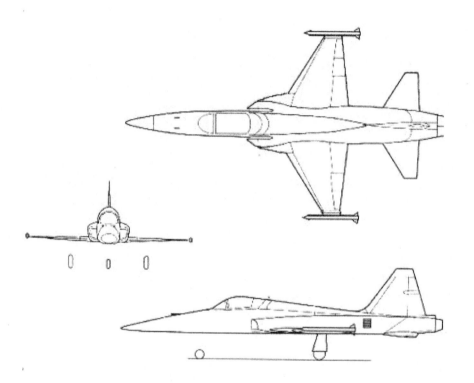

General Electric J-85 Comparison Data

Specification	F-5A/B J-85-GE-13	F-5E J-85-GE-21
Length inches	105.6 Inches	112.5
Diameter inches	21 inches	21
Weight (Dry) pounds	597 pounds	684
Maximum Thrust pounds	4,085 pounds	5,000
Military Thrust pounds	2,850 pounds	3,500
Compressor Stages	8	9
Pressure Ratio	7:1	8.3:1
Mass Air Flow pounds/second	44 pounds/second	53
Specific Fuel Consumption pounds	1.03 pounds	1.00

In 1954, General Electric Aircraft Engines developed the J-85 turbojet engine. Production of the various versions of this engine lasted until 1988. Approximately 13,600 of these engines were delivered to various customers.

General Electric J-85 Improvements

F-5E/F Aircraft

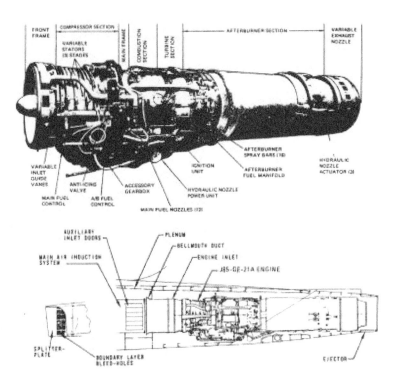

The engine in the original Skoshi Tiger aircraft was sufficient to propel the aircraft to Mach 1.4. However, due to lessons learned during the combat evaluation of the aircraft in Vietnam, Northrop and General Electric worked to improve the power plant/airframe interface. The J-85-GE-21 engine was the result of that effort. The improved engine produced significantly more thrust (over 900 pounds more) than the Skoshi Tigers J-85-GE-13 engine. Also improved were reliability and maintainability. The new engine required less maintenance man –hours per flight hour to maintain. Airframe mounted auxiliary inlet doors on the F-5E provided greater airflow to the engine when required.

Acknowledgements

The author recognizes that some words, model names and designations mentioned in this book are the property of the trademark holder. They are used as definition only. This is not an official publication. The author wishes to thank each of the following individuals and organizations for the contribution of time and information:

HQ. USAF Historical Research Center

Research Division

Maxwell AFB, Al

AFHSO/HOS

Reference & Analysis Division

Bolling AFB, Washington, DC

A special thanks to Thanh (Tom) Duong for information provided

Index

Printed in Great Britain
by Amazon

21810676R00066